INTRODUCTORY ASSYRIAN GRAMMAR

Samuel A. B. Mercer

DOVER PUBLICATIONS, INC.
MINEOLA, NEW YORK

TO FRITZ HOMMEL

Scholar, Teacher, and Friend

Bibliographical Note

This Dover edition, first published in 2003, is an unabridged republication of the work originally published in 1961 by Frederick Ungar Publishing Co., New York, under the title *Assyrian Grammar with Chrestomathy and Glossary.*

Library of Congress Cataloging-in-Publication Data

Mercer, Samuel A. B. (Samuel Alfred Browne), b. 1880.
[Assyrian grammar]
Introductory Assyrian grammar / Samuel A. B. Mercer.
p. cm.
Originally published: Assyrian grammar. New York : F. Ungar, 1961.
ISBN 0-486-42815-X
1. Akkadian language—Grammar. 2. Akkadian language—Readers I. Title.

PJ3251 .M6 2003
492'.182421—dc21

2002190839

Manufactured in the United States of America
Dover Publications, Inc., 31 East 2nd Street, Mineola, N.Y. 11501

PREFACE

Experience in teaching Semitic languages has taught me that the beginner needs a text-book which is both simple and also well supplied with exercises. Hitherto no such book for the study of Assyrian has appeared in any modern language. There are books in English, French, German and Italian for beginners, but none of them are provided with exercises. The larger grammars are reference books and unsuited for the use of beginners. The book most generally used in the study of the Assyrian language is DELITZSCH's *Assyrische Lesestücke*. But everyone complains of its difficulty for the beginner.

Assyrian is difficult. Nor have compilers of Assyrian grammars done much to make it attractive to the student. It is with this in mind that I have prepared this little book. I have divided the grammar and syntax into chapters or lessons, and supplied each chapter with copious exercises. I am sure that if the student works through these lessons with care and diligence he will have no trouble with the reading exercises which follow.

The beginner should first *memorise* the *Simple Syllables.* These are fundamental and occur most frequently in all cuneiform texts. He should *read* chapter two with care, and so acquaint himself with the *Ideograms* as to be able easily to refer to them in his later work. Chapter three should also be *read* with care, looking up each sign in the Sign List at the end of the book. Chapter four is for further practice in the Sign List. The aim thus far has been to acquaint the student with his signs. A careful *reading* of chapter five is all that is necessary. But the pronouns, verbs, nouns, adjectives, numerals, adverbs, prepositions and conjunctions, chapters six to twenty-seven, should be ***committed to memory***, and the exercises on each lesson should by carefully read. Read the Syntax carefully and do the exercises with diligence. After the Chrestomathy is finished the student should read some of the longer passages in DELITZSCH's *Lesestücke* (which he should own), and then he will be prepared, with the assistance of BRÜNNOW, *A Classified List*, Leyden, 1889, and DELITZSCH's *Assyrisches Handwörterbuch*, Leipzig, 1896, for independent reading.

The author's object has been to make this book as brief and concise as possible. He warns students against thinking that they can acquire an adequate knowledge of Assyrian without much memory-work. If the above directions are followed, the author feels that the object for which the book has been prepared will be attained — namely, to add to the number of students interested in the study of Assyrian.

It remains only to thank my pupil, Mr. KELLER, for arranging the vocabulary, and to express my appreciation of the excellent work done by the *Akademische Buchdruckerei F. Straub*, Munich. For many hints I have to thank my former teacher, Professor HOMMEL, who also very kindly read the proof.

Samuel A. B. Mercer

Hibbard Egyptian Library,
Western Theological Seminary,
Chicago.

May 10, 1921.

CONTENTS

GRAMMAR

SYNTAX

GRAMMAR

INTRODUCTION

§ 1. Assyrian belongs to the northern group of Semitic languages, and is closely related to the Hebrew. Its differences from Babylonian are only dialectical. The Assyro-Babylonian language was used as early, at least, as 3000 B.C. and continued in vogue until the first century before the Christian era. From that time until 1835 A.D. when Sir HENRY C. RAWLINSON made the first partial translation of an Assyrian text, the Assyrian language was quite unknown. Since then thousands of inscriptions on stone and clay have been excavated from the buried cities of the Tigris-Euphrates valley.

The literature of the Assyro-Babylonian inscriptions is voluminous, and much more awaits the industry of the archaeologist. All types of literature are represented. There are poetry and prose, prayers and hymns, incantations and magical charms, chronology and history, precepts and laws, and legal and commercial transactions. Thousands of texts have been translated, and there still remain thousands untranslated in published or unpublished form. Work upon these texts is still in its infancy. Fuller sign lists must be made, better dictionaries must be written, and new grammatical points remain to be investigated. All this must be done in order that the student of history, religion, morals, politics, science, and social institutions may have the means of defining the slow developement of Semitic ideas throughout the centuries.

Every student of Assyrian should read an account of the decipherment of the script and of the reconstruction of the language, and no more fascinating story of that great achievement can be found than that in R. W. ROGER's A History of Babylonia and Assyria, Vol. I, pp. 1—353.*) Of translations of texts there are numerous volumes, but so far there is no complete corpus of Assyro-Babylonian literature, nor can there be such for many years to come. The most complete at present is the Vorderasiatische Bibliothek, published by HINRICHS in Leipzig. It was begun in 1907 and is still in progress. There is nothing similar to this in any other modern language, although the Yale University Press have in view a corpus which will be complete to date. Of individual books in which translations of Assyro-Babylonian texts are published there are many, which can be found in any good university or seminary library.

*) See also FRITZ HOMMEL, Geschichte Babyloniens und Assyriens, Berlin 1885, p. 58—134 and H. V. HILPRECHT, Explorations in Bible Lands during the 19th century, Philadelphia 1903, p. 3—577 (p. 3—213 also in German translation: Die Ausgrabungen in Assyrien und Babylonien, I., Bis zum Auftreten De Sarzec's, Leipzig 1904).

CHAPTER I

SIMPLE SYLLABLES

§ 2. The name whereby the script of the Assyrian language is known is cuneiform. The word is derived from the Latin, *cuneus*, a wedge and *forma*, a form, wedge-form. The script was originally pictographic and was handed on by the Sumerians to the Semites who lived in the Tigris-Euphrates valley. In later times it was used by many peoples other than the Assyro-Babylonians, and was at last highly simplified and used by the Persians.

The Assyro-Babylonians never developed an alphabet. There are a few vowel signs, but the script is mostly syllabic. The signs are written from left to right.

In this first lesson, about a hundred of the simplest syllabic signs are arranged according to the order of the Hebrew alphabet. This is the order in which the transliterated words occur in all Assyrian glossaries and dictionaries. On the left-hand side syllables beginning with a consonant are arranged, those with a final *a* being placed in the first column, those with *i* or *e* in the second and those with *u* in the third. On the right-hand side syllables beginning with a vowel are recorded, first those with *a*, secondly those with *i* or *e* and thirdly those with *u* It is very important that all these signs with their values be thoroughly committed to memory. In section 4 these same syllabic signs are arranged in the order in which all these and other signs are found in all sign lists. This exercise should be carefully studied. The signs should be read and repeatedly written until they are as well known as an alphabet.

Final Vowel

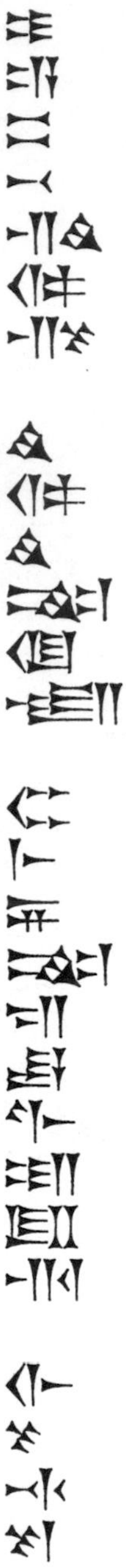
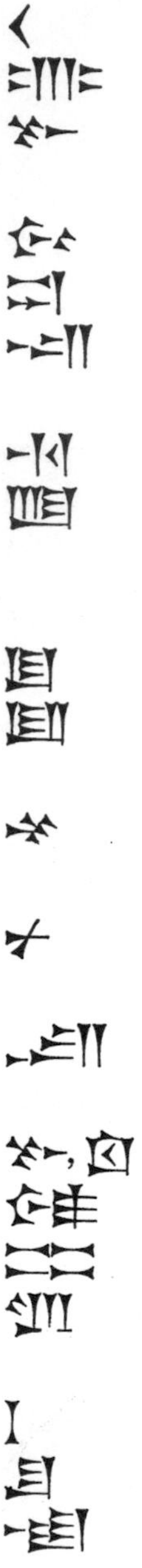

§ 3.	א	A		= *a*		= *i*		= *u*
						= *e*		= *ú*
	ב	B		= *ba*		= *bi*		= *bu*
						= *be*		
	ג	G		= *ga*		= *gi*		= *gu*
	ד	D		= *da*		= *di*		= *du*
	ז	Z		= *za*		= *zi*		= *zu*
	א, ה							
	ח	Ḫ		= *ḫa*		= *ḫi*		= *ḫu*
	ט	Ṭ		= *ṭa*		= *ṭi*		= *ṭu*
						= *ṭi*		
						= *ṭe*		
	כ	K		= *ka*		= *ki*		= *ku*
	ל	L		= *la*		= *li*		= *lu*
	מ	M		= *ma*		= *mi*		= *mu*
						= *me*		
	נ	N		= *na*		= *ni*		= *nu*
						= *ne*		
	ס	S		= *sa*		= *si*		= *su*
						= *se*		[*pú*
	פ	P		= *pa*		= *pi*		= *pu*,
	צ	Ṣ		= *ṣa*		= *ṣi*		= *ṣu*
	ק	Ḳ		= *ḳa*		= *ḳi*		= *ḳu*
	ר	R		= *ra*		= *ri*		= *ru*
	ש	Š		= *šá*		= *ši*		= *šu*
				= *ša*		= *še*		= *šú*
	ת	T		= *ta*		= *ti*		= *tu*
						= *te*		

Initial Vowel

= *ab*	= *ib*	= *ub*
= *ag*	= *ig*	= *ug*
= *ad*	= *id*	= *ud*
= *az*	= *iz*	= *uz*
= *a'*	= *i'*	= *u'*
= *aḫ*	= *iḫ*	= *uḫ*
= *aṭ*	= *iṭ*	= *uṭ*
= *ak*	= *ik*	= *uk*
= *al*	= *il*	= *ul*
	= *el*	
= *am*	= *im*	= *um*
= *an*	= *in*	= *un*
	= *en*	
= *as*	= *is*	= *us*
= *ap*	= *ip*	= *up*
= *aṣ*	= *iṣ*	= *uṣ*
= *aḳ*	= *iḳ*	= *uḳ*
= *ar*	= *ir*	= *ur*
= *ár*	= *er*	= *úr*
= *aš*	= *iš*	= *uš*
= *áš*	= *eš*	
= *at*	= *it*	= *ut*

§ 4. Read and write:

CHAPTER II

OTHER SYLLABLES, IDEOGRAMS AND DETERMINATIVES

§ 5. In addition to the *simple syllables*, illustrated in chapter I, there were also *compound* (or better *fuller*) *syllables*, e. g. , *bit*; , *dan*; , *ḫar*; , *man*.

In Assyrian it was not easy to represent long and short vowels. In open syllables, long vowels were represented in one of two ways, namely, (1) By writing after a syllable a separate sign for the vowel of the syllable, e. g. , *na-a* = *nā*; , *la-a* = *lā*. But such a separate sign was not always written, e. g. = *nā*. (2) By doubling the consonant, e. g. , *ru-uḳ-ḳu* i. e. *rūḳu*. In closed syllables it was practically impossible to represent a long vowel.

§ 6. Sometimes the Assyrians used one sign to represent a complete word. This we call an *ideogram*, e. g. , as a syllable, has the value of *an*, but as a word, or ideogram, has the value *ilu*, which means "god". Likewise, 𒀜, as a syllable, equals *ad*; as an ideogram, equals *abu*, "father".

An ideogram may consist of two or more signs, e. g. 𒀊𒍪, *apsû*, "abyss"; 𒍪𒈝𒈠, *suluppu*, "date".

Many signs have more than one syllabic value, as well as more than one ideographic value, e. g. 𒌓 has the syllabic values *ud*, *tu*, *tam*, *pir*, *laḫ*, *ḫis*; and the ideographic values *ûmu*, "day", *šamšu*, "sun", and *piṣû*, "white".

§ 7. An ideogram may also be used as a *determinative*, that is, a sign attached to a word to indicate the *class of thing* to which the word belongs. Most of the determinatives are placed before the words to which they refer; and are not pronounced, e. g. 𒀭, before names of deities, 𒁹, before male proper nouns; 𒆳, before names of countries and mountains.

§ 8. Many ideograms have no determinatives. In order to help in identifying the correct ideographic value of a sign a device was used by the Assyrians, which we call a *phonetic complement*; e. g. the sign 𒀭, as an ideogram, is used for both *ilu*, "god", and *šamû*, "heaven". In order to help the reader to decide which, the Assyrian would add the sign 𒂊, *e*, when he wished to represent *šame*, "heavens", thus, 𒀭 𒂊.

§ 9. As an exercise, read and write the following *ideograms* and *determinatives*. Become so acquainted with them that future reference to them may be made with ease.

IDEOGRAMS

Ideogram	*Pronunciation*	*Meaning*
𒋻	*nakâsu*	to cut off
𒆰	*zêru*	seed, descendant
𒈬	*šumu*	name
𒀭	*ilu*	god

Ideogram	*Pronunciation*	*Meaning*
	balāṭu	life
	ardu	slave
	palū	reign, year of reign
	paṭru	dagger
	ṣīru	exalted
	alu	city
	taḫāzu	battle
	arḫu	month
	rubū	noble
	napištu	life, soul
	iṣṣūru	bird
	bašū	to be
	šumēlu	left
	bēlu	lord
	ḳātu	hand
	zumru	body
	rēšu	beginning
	pū	mouth
	lišānu	tongue
	nakru	hostile
	ṣalmu	image
	epēšu	to make
	ḫarrānu	road
	šikaru	strong drink
	abnu	stone
	šarru	king

Ideogram	*Pronunciation*	*Meaning*
	*šīru*	flesh
	*išātu*	fire
	*ṣiḫru*	small
	*ummu*	mother
	*bābu*	gate
	*kakkabu*	star
	*dūru*	wall
	*nadānu*	to give
	*alāku*	to go
	*imēru*	ass
	*karānu*	wine
	*duppu*	tablet
	*abu*	father
	iṣu	wood
	*alpu*	ox
	*kibratu*	region, quarter of heaven
	*dannu*	mighty
	*nišu*	people
	*sukkallu*	messenger
	*bītu*	house, temple
	*imnu*	right
	*amēlu*	man
	*aḫu*	brother
	*idu*	side
	*ḳablu*	midst, battle
	*rabū*	great

Ideogram	*Pronunciation*	*Meaning*
	parakku	shrine
	mātu	land
	ṣiru	serpent
	ūmu	day
	uznu	ear
	libbu	heart
	ṣābu	warrior
	ṭābu	good
	šāru	wind
	mūšu	night
	kiššatu	host, the world
	šēpu	foot
	murṣu	sickness
	īnu	eye
	damḳu	favourable
	šarāpu	to burn
	limnu	evil
	irṣitu	earth
	ellu	bright
	šarru	king
	ṣubātu	garment
	išū	to have
	libittu	brick
	aššatu	wife
	bēltu	lady
	aplu	son (spec. heir)

Ideogram	*Pronunciation*	*Meaning*
	šakānu	to set
	nūnu	fish

COMPOUND IDEOGRAMS

	elū	high
	apsū	abyss
	ešēru	to be straight, right
	suluppu	date
	šuttu	dream
	abullu	city-gate
	ekallu	palace
	šaplū	low
	purussū	decision
	zunnu	rain
	eḳlu	field
	dimtu	weeping

DETERMINATIVES THAT PRECEDE THE WORD

	ilu	god	before names of deities
	alu	city	„ „ „ cities
	arḫu	month	„ „ „ months
	šīru	flesh	„ „ „ parts of the body
	kakkabu	star	„ „ „ stars and planets
	imēru	ass	„ „ „ some of the larger animals

abnu	stone	before names of stones
iṣu	wood	" " " trees, wooden objects
karpatu	vessel	" " " vessels
šammu	plant	" " " plants
amēlu	man	" " " tribes and professions
mātu	country	" " " countries
šadū	mountain	" " " mountains
	male	" " " male proper names
ṣubātu	garment	" " " garments and stuffs
immeru	lamb, sheep	" " " sheep
šipātu	fleece, wool	" " " wools and woolen stuffs
nāru	river	" " " rivers
	female	" " " female proper nouns .

DETERMINATIVES THAT FOLLOW THE WORD

kám	used after numbers
kam	" " "
plural	" " plurals
ta-a-an	" " numbers and measures
ki	" " names of places (comp. *ašru* place)
plural	" " plurals
a-an	" " numerals and measures
nūnu fish	" " names of fish
iṣṣūru bird	" " " " birds

CHAPTER III

SIGN LIST

§ 10. The sign list at the end of the book, immediately before the Glossary, should now be carefully studied. It cannot be learned all at once, but will come with practice.

§ 11. For practice in finding signs in the Sign List the following words should be carefully read. In order to show the close relationship between Assyrian and Hebrew, the Hebrew equivalent of each Assyrian word is given.

ba-nu-u	to build	בָּנָה
sa-ḫa-pu	to overwhelm	סָחַף
la-ba-šú	to clothe	לָבַשׁ
la-ma-du	to learn	לָמַד
la-ḳu-u	to take	לָקַח
li-ša-a-nu	tongue	לָשׁוֹן
šú-mu	name	שֵׁם
be-e-lu	lord	בַּעַל
na-piš-tu	life	נֶפֶשׁ
na-aš-ru	eagle	נֶשֶׁר
na-a-ru	river	נָהָר
ḳa-nu-u	reed	קָנֶה
ḳa-aš-tu	bow	קֶשֶׁת
ti-ib-nu	straw	תֶּבֶן
aḳ-ra-bu	scorpion	עַקְרָב
zi-e-ru	seed	זֶרַע
dal-tu	door	דֶּלֶת
ri-e-šu	head	ראשׁ
ab-nu	stone	אֶבֶן

um-mu	mother	אֵם
i-nu	eye	עַיִן
i-du	hand, side	יָד
i-lu	god	אֵל
i-ṣu	wood	עֵץ
i-ša-tu	fire	אֵשׁ
i-ša-ru	righteous	יָשָׁר
at-ta	thou	אַתָּה
kak-ka-bu	star	כּוֹכָב
mal-ku	prince	מֶלֶךְ
ir-šú	couch	עֶרֶשׂ
ir-ṣi-tu	earth	אֶרֶץ
am-tu	handmaid	אָמָה
bi-i-tu	house	בַּיִת
ḳu-u-lu	cry	קוֹל
zik-ru	name	זֵכֶר
al-pu	ox	אֶלֶף
e-mu	father-in-law	חָם
e-zi-bu	to leave	עָזַב
e-pi-ru	dust	עָפָר
e-ṭi-ru	to protect	עָטַר
e-lu-u	to be high	עָלָה
kal-bu	dog	כֶּלֶב
ra-ka-bu	to ride	רָכַב
ṭa-a-bu	good	טוֹב
ḳar-nu	horn	קֶרֶן
ma-ḫa-ṣu	to smite	מָחַץ

gam-ma-lu	camel	גָּמָל
uz-nu	ear	אֹזֶן
*u-mu**)	day	יוֹם
pi-tu-u	to open	פָּתַח
lib-bu	heart	לֵבָב
im-nu	right hand	יָמִין
bir-ḳu	lightning	בָּרָק
bir-ku	knee	בֶּרֶךְ
ar-ba-ʾ-u	four	אַרְבַּע
di-i-nu	judgment	דִּין
ib-ru	friend	חָבֵר
ḳin-nu	nest	קֵן
a-ḫu	brother	אָח
a-ri-bu	raven	עֹרֵב
a-na-ku	I	אָנֹכִי
a-bu	father	אָב
a-ḫa-zu	to seize	אָחַז
ṣa-al-mu	image	צֶלֶם
ḫa-ta-nu	son-in-law	חָתָן
ḫa-du-ú	to rejoice	חָדָה
ša-am-nu	oil	שֶׁמֶן

*) Or better *ūmu(-mu)* i. e. *ūmu* (comp. p. 10, line 5) with phonetic complement (p. 7, § 8) *-mu*.

CHAPTER IV

SYLLABARIES

§ 12. For further practice, before going on to the study of the grammar proper, a small portion of each of the three great syllabaries, S^a, S^b and S^c, is given. These syllabaries were composed by the Babylonians and Assyrians themselves, and have been of inestimable value to modern students in reconstructing the grammar and lexicon of the Sumerian and of the Assyrian language.

§ 13. *Syllabary S^a.* In the second column is the syllable under consideration, in the first column the pronunciation of the syllable, and in the third column the name of the syllabic sign.

§ 14. *Syllabary S^b.* In the second column is the ideogram under consideration, in the first column the Sumerian pronunciation, and in the third column the Assyrian translation of the ideographic sign.

§ 15. *Syllabary S^c.* This is in a sense a combination of S^a and S^b. In the second column is the ideogram under consideration, in the first column the pronunciation of the same, in the third column the name of the ideographic sign, and in the fourth column the Assyrian translation with synonyms.

CHAPTER V

PHONOLOGY

§ 16. *Vowels.* The Assyrian language possesses the vowels *a*, *i*, *u*, *ā*, *ī*, *ū*, and *e* as a variant sound of *i* and *a*, and *o* as a variant sound of *u*.

The vowels *a* and *ā* change to *e*, *ē*, and *ī*, e. g. *i-ma-a-ru* into *i-me-e-ru*; *mu-ša-ak-ni-šú* into *mu-ši-ik-ni-šú*.

Vocal contraction is common, e. g. *ba-nu-u* for *ba-ni-u*.

Vowels sometimes fall off, e. g. *šú-ub-tu* for *u-šú-ub-tu*.

§ 17. *Consonants.*

The Assyrian consonants are: *b*, *g*, *d*, *z*, *ḫ*, *ṭ*, *k*, *l*, *m*, *n*, *s*, *p*, *ṣ*, *ḳ(q)*, *r*, *š*, *t*. These consonants are arranged according to the Hebrew order.

The consonant *k* after *n* or *m* sometimes becomes *g*, e. g. *lu-uš-kum-ga* for *lu-uš-kum-ka*.

Sometimes *ḳ* is replaced by *g*, e. g. *gātu* for *ḳātu*.

Before a dental *m* becomes *n*, e. g. *ša-li-in-tu* for *ša-li-im-tu*; also before *š*, e. g. *šú-un-šu* for *šú-um-šu*.

After *n*, *t* often changes to *d*, e. g. *un-da-aš-šir* for *um-ta-aš-šir*; after *ḳ* it changes to *ṭ*, e. g. *iḳ-ṭe-bi* for *iḳ-te-bi*.

In some verbal forms *št* and *ṣt* become *ss* and *ṣṣ*, e. g. *as-sa-kan* for *aš-ta-kan*; *aṣ-ṣa-bat* for *aṣ-ta-bat*.

Sibilants change to *l* before a dental, e. g. *al-ṭu-ur* for *aš-ṭu-ur*; or before sibilants, e. g. *al-sī* for *aš-sī*.

After a dental or another sibilant *š* becomes *s*, with which the preceding sibilant, and sometimes the dental, assimilate, e. g. *ḳāt-su*, *ḳa-as-su*, or *ḳa-a-su* for *ḳāt-šu*.

Before certain consonants *n* changes to *m*, e. g. *u-šam-kir**) for *u-šan-kir*; but usually it assimilates, e. g. *id-din* for *in-din*.

§ 18. *Accent.*

As yet very little is known about Assyrian accentuation. Monosyllables are accented, e. g. *šár mātāti.* When the last syllable is long it is accented, e. g. *šarrût māt Aššur.*

The accent recedes till it finds a long or closed syllable, e. g. *šarrûtu, ínnamir.*

In some forms a short penultima is accented, e. g. *ikášad.*

The enclitics *-mā* and *-ni* drive the accent back upon the penultima, e. g. *ibnûmā, iprusûni.*

§ 19. *Exercises.*

[illegible]

*) More correct is the transscription *ú-šán-kir.*

CHAPTER VI
PERSONAL PRONOUN

§ 20. The personal pronouns in the *nominative* are:

	Singular	Plural
1 c.	*anāku*	*anīni, anīnu, nīnu, nīni*
2 m.	*atta*	*attunu*
2 f.	*attī*	
3 m.	*šū*	*šūnu, šun*
3 f.	*šī*	*šīna, šin*

§ 21. The personal pronouns in the *genitive* and *accusative* are:

	Singular	Plural
1 c.	*iātu, iāti, iāši, a-a-ši*	*niāti, niāšim, nāši*
2 m.	*kātu, kāti, kāša*	*kātunu, kāšunu*
2 f.	*kāti, kāši*	
3 m.	*šāšu, šuāšu*	*šāšúnu, šāšun*
3 f.	*šāša, šāši*	

§ 22. Pronominal suffixes attached to nouns with *possessive* meaning:

	Singular	Plural
1 c.	*-ī, -ia, -a*	*-ni, -nu*
2 m.	*-ka, -ku*	*-kunū, -kun*
2 f.	*-ki*	[*-kinā*]
3 m.	*-šú, -š, -ša*	*-šúnu, -šún, -šúnūti*
3 f.	*-ša*	*-šina, -šin*

§ 23. Pronominal suffixes attached to verbs with *accusative* meaning:

	Singular	Plural
1 c.	*-anni, -inni, -ni*	*-nāši, -annāši, -annāšu*
2 m.	*-ka, -akka, -ikka, -ak, -akku*	*-kunūši, -akkunūšu*
2 f.	*-ki, -akki, -ikki*	*-kināši*
3 m.	*-šú, -š, -aššu, -aš*	*-šunu, -aššunu, -šunūtu, -šunūti*
3 f.	*-ši, -š, -ašši*	*-šina, -šinātu, -šināti, -šināšim, -aššinātu, -aššinīti*

§ 24. *Exercises.*

[illegible]

CHAPTER VII

OTHER PRONOUNS

§ 25. *Demonstrative Pronouns.* There are five chief demonstrative pronouns:

1. *annū*, this

	Singular		Plural	
	masc.	fem.	masc.	fem.
nom.	*annū*	*annītu*	*annūtu*	*annātu*
	anniu		*an(n)ūte*	*annāte*
				annītu
gen.	*annē*	*annīti*		*annīti*
acc.	*annā*	*annīta*		

2. *šuātu*, that

šuātu(m)	*šiāti*	*šuātunu*	*šuātina*
šuāti(m)		*šātunu*	*šātina*
šūtu		*šunūti*	*šinātina*
šātu			*šināti*

	Singular masc.	Singular fem.	Plural masc.	Plural fem.
3. *šū*, that				
	šū	*šī*		
4. *ammū*, that				
	ammū	*ammētu*		*ammāle*
5. *ullū*, that				
nom.	*ullū*		*ullūtu*	
gen.	*ulli* (*ullē*)			

§ 26. *Relative Pronouns.*

1. *ša*, who, which.
2. *man(n)u ša*, whoever.
3. *minū*, *minma ša*, *mim(m)a (ša)*, *mimmū*, whatever.
4. *mal(a)*, *ammar*, as many as.

§ 27. *Interrogative Pronouns.*

1. *mannu*, who?

masc.		neut.
mannu	nom.	*minū*
	gen.	*minē*
	acc.	*minā*

2. *a-a-ú* (i. e. *ai-ú*), who?; fem. *a-a-ta*; plural *aiiūtu*, *aiiuti*.

§ 28. *Indefinite Pronouns.*

1. Masculine: *manman*, *mamman*, *manuman*, *mam(m)ana*, *memēni*, *manāma*, *manamma*, *manma*, *mam(m)a*, *mumma*, anyone.

   Neuter: *minma*, *mim(m)a*, *mimmu*, *aiiumma*, *aiiamma*, *iaumma*, anything.

§ 29. *Reflexive Pronoun.* This is expressed by the word *ramānu*, self.

§ 30. *Exercises.*

CHAPTER VIII

THE STRONG VERB

§ 31. *The Skeleton of the Strong Verb.* The Assyrian verb has ordinarily four primary, three secondary, and one tertiary stem. The model verb ***kašādu*** means to conquer.

1.			2.		
I 1 (or o, 1)	Qal	***ikášad***	I 2 (or t, 1)	Ifteal	***iktášad***
II 1 (or o, 2)	Paal	***ukaššad***	II 2 (or t, 2)	Iftaal	***uktaššad***
III 1 (or s, 1)	Shafal	***ušakšad***	III 2 (or st, 1)	Ishtafal	***uštakšad***
IV 1 (or n, 1)	Nifal	***ikkášad***			

3.

I 3 (or tn, 1) Iftaneal ***iktanášad***

1. There are other stems which are not of very frequent occurrence. Such are: IV 2 (or nt, 1), Ittafal; II 3 (or tn, 2), Iftanaal; III 3 (or stn, 1), Ishtanafal; IV 3 (or ntn, 1), Ittanafal; III/II 1 (or s, 2), Ishpaal; and III/II 2 (or st, 2), Ishtapaal.

2. These stems are referred to as, Qal, Paal, Shafal, etc., or, more conveniently as, I_1, II_1, III_1, IV_1, I_2, II_2, etc.

3. The signification and formation of the various stems:

I_1, *Qal* is the root stem, used transitively and intransitively.

II_1, *Paal* signifies intensity, and has its middle consonant doubled.

III_1, *Shafal* has a causative signification, and is formed by prefixing the consonant *š*.

IV_1, *Nifal* is passive in signification, and is formed by prefixing the consonant *n*, which is sometimes changed to accord with the first consonant of the root.

I_2, *Ifteal* is reflexive in signification. It is derived from the Qal.

II_2, *Iftaal* has both active and passive signification. It is derived from the Paal.

III_2, *Ishtafal* is a reflexive of the causative. It is derived from the Shafal.

IV_2, *Ittafal* has a passive signification, and is derived from the Nifal. Originally *Intafal.*

I_3, *Iftaneal*; II_3, *Iftanaal*; III_3, *Ishtanafal*; and IV_3, *Ittanafal* are derived from I_2, II_2, III_2, and IV_2, respectively, and are similar in meaning.

III/II_1, *Ishpaal*; and III/II_2, *Ishtapaal* are similar in signification to the Shafal and Ishtafal, respectively. They are a Paal-Shafal and a Paal-Ishtafal, respectively.

4. The Assyrian verb in usually tri-consonantal, e. g. ***kašādu***, but there are also roots with two and sometimes four consonants. These consonants are called ***radicals***.

§ 32. *Vocabulary.*

damāḳu	= to be favourable	***rakābu***	= to ride
kašādu	= to conquer	***šakānu***	= to place.

§ 33. *Exercises.*

CHAPTER IX

§ 34. *The Qal, or* I_1.

PRESENT

	Singular	Plural
3 m.	*ikašad* (*ikaššad*)	*ikašadū(ni/u)*
3 f.	*takašad*	*ikašadā(ni)*
2 m.	*takašad*	*takašadū*
2 f.	*takašadī*	*takašadā*
1 c.	*akašad*	*nikašad*

PRETERITE

3 m.	*ikšud*	*ikšudū(ni/u)*
3 f.	*takšud*	*ikšudā(ni)*
2 m.	*takšud*	*takšudū*
2 f.	*takšudī*	*takšudā*
1 c.	*akšud*	*nikšud*

PERMANSIVE

3 m.	*kašid*	*kašdū(ni)*
3 f.	*kašdat*, *kašdāt(a)*	*kašdā(ni)*
2 m.	*kašdāt(a)*	*kašdātunu*
2 f.	*kašdāti*	[*kašdātina*]
1 c.	*kašdāk(u)*	*kašdāni(-nu)*

IMPERATIVE

2 m.	*kušud*	*kušudū*
2 f.	*kušudī*	*kušudā(ni)*

PARTICIPLE	INFINITIVE
kaš(i)du	*kašādu*

The Assyrian verb has three tenses: Present, preterite and permansive. The present expresses incomplete action and is rendered in English by the present or future. The preterite expresses complete action and is rendered by the English imperfect, perfect or pluperfect. The permansive resembles a noun or participle, and takes suffixes. It expresses a state or condition; thus, *ša-ak-nu-u-ni*, they are set.

§ 36. *Vocabulary.*

palāḫu = to fear
katāmu = to cover
zakāru = to speak
ṣabātu = to grasp
labāšu = to clothe.
ḳarābu = to draw near
kanāšu = to submit
paṭāru = to release
labāru = to be old

§ 37. *Exercises.*

CHAPTER X

§ 38. *The Paal, or* II_1.

PRESENT

	Singular	Plural
3 m.	*ukaššad*	*ukaššadū(ni)*
3 f.	*tukaššad*	*ukaššadā(ni)*
2 m.	*tukaššad*	*tukaššadū*
2 f.	*tukaššadī*	*tukaššadā*
1 c.	*ukaššad*	*nukaššad*

PRETERITE

	Singular	Plural
3 m.	*ukaššid*	*ukaššidū(ni)*
3 f.	*tukaššid*	*ukaššidā(ni)*
2 m.	*tukaššid*	*tukaššidū*
2 f.	*tukaššidī*	*tukaššidā*
1 c.	*ukaššid*	*nukaššid*

PERMANSIVE

	Singular	Plural
3 m.	*kuššud*	*kuššudū(ni)*
3 f.	*kuššudat*	*kuššudā*
2 m.	*kuššudāt(a)*	*kuššudātunu*
2 f.	*kuššudāti*	?
1 c.	*kuššudāk(u)*	*kuššudāni*

IMPERATIVE

	Singular	Plural
2 m.	*kuššid*, *kaššid*	*kuššidū*
2 f.	*kuššidī*	*kuššidā*

PARTICIPLE	INFINITIVE
mukaššidu	*kuššudu*

39. *The Shafal, or* III_1.

PRESENT

	Singular	Plural
3 m.	*ušakšad*	*ušakšadū(ni)*
3 f.	*tušakšad*	*ušakšadā(ni)*
2 m.	*tušakšad*	*tušakšadū*
2 f.	*tušākšadī*	*tušakšadā*
1 c.	*ušakšad*	*nušakšad*

PRETERITE

	Singular	Plural
3 m.	*ušakšid*	*ušakšidū(ni)*
3 f.	*tušakšid*	*ušakšidā(ni)*
2 m.	*tušakšid*	*tušakšidū*
2 f.	*tušakšidī*	*tušakšidā*
1 c.	*ušakšid*	*nušakšid*

PERMANSIVE

3 m.	*šukšud*	*šukšudū(ni)*
3 f.	*šukšudat*	*šukšudā*
2 m.	*šukšudāta*	*šukšudātunu*
2 f.	*šukšudāti*	?
1 c.	*šukšudāk(u)*	*šukšudāni*

IMPERATIVE

2 m.	*šukšid*	*šukšidū*
2 f.	*šukšidī*	*šukšidā*

PARTICIPLE

mušakšidu

INFINITIVE

šukšudu

§ 40. *The Nifal, or* IV_1.

PRESENT

3 m.	*ikkašad*	*ikkašadū(ni)*
3 f.	*takkašad*	*ikkašadā(ni)*
2 m.	*takkašad*	*takkašadū*
2 f.	*takkašadī*	*takkašadā*
1 c.	*akkašad*	*nikkašad*

PRETERITE

3 m.	*ikkašid*	*ikkašidū(ni)*
3 f.	*takkašid*	*ikkašidā(ni)*
2 m.	*takkašid*	*takkašidū*
2 f.	*takkašidī*	*takkašidā*
1 c.	*akkašid*	*nikkašid*

PERMANSIVE

	Singular	Plural
3 m.	*nakšud*	*nakšudū(ni)*
3 f.	*nakšudat*	*nakšudā*
2 m.	*nakšudāta*	*nakšudātunu*
2 f.	*nakšudāti*	?
1 c.	*nakšudāk(u)*	*nakšudāni*

IMPERATIVE

2 m.	*nakšid*	*nakšidū*
2 f.	*nakšidī*	*nakšidā*

PARTICIPLE

mukkašidu

INFINITIVE

nakšudu, nakašudu

41. *Exercises.*

CHAPTER XI

§ 42. *The Derived Stems.*

	IFTEAL, OR I_2	IFTAAL, OR II_2	ISHTAFAL, OR III_2	IFTANEAL, OR I_3
PRESENT	*iktašad*	*uktaššad*	*uštakšad*	*iktanašad*
PRETERITE	*iktašad*	*uktaššid*, *uktēšid*	*uštakšid*, *ušteksid*	*iktanašad*
PERMANSIVE	*kitašud*, *kitšud*	*kutaššud*	*šutakšud*	
IMPERATIVE	*kitašad*, *kitšad*		*šutakšid*	
PARTICIPLE	*muktašidu*	*muktaššidu*	*muštakšidu*	
INFINITIVE	*kitašudu*, *kitšudu*	*kutaššudu*	*šutakšudu*	

After learning the four principal stems, the student will find no difficulty in filling in these conjugations.

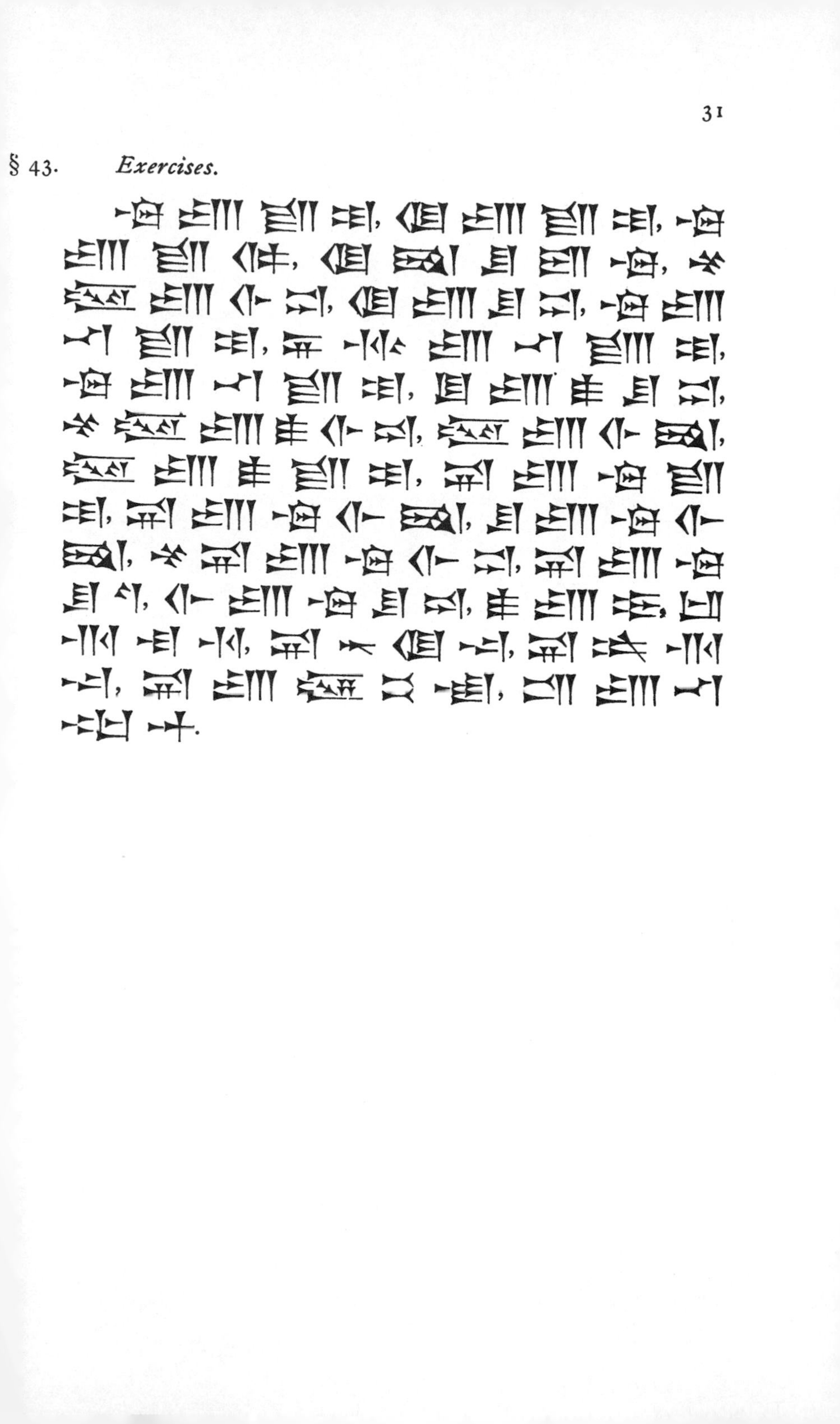

§ 43. *Exercises.*

CHAPTER XII

§ 44. *Synopsis of the Strong Verb.*

	QAL	PAAL	SHAFEL	NIFAL	IFTEAL	IFTAAL	ISHTAFAL	IFTANEAL
PRESENT	*ikašad*	*ukaššad*	*ušakšad*	*ikkašad*	*iktašad*	*uktaššad*	*uštakšad*	*iktanašad*
PRETERITE	*ikšud*	*ukaššid*	*ušakšid*	*ikkašid*	*iktašad*	*uktaššid*	*uštakšid*	*iktanašad*
PERMANSIVE	*kašid*	*kuššud*	*šukšud*	*nakšud*	*kitašud*	*kutaššud*	*šutakšud*	
IMPERATIVE	*kušud*	*kuššid*	*šukšid*	*nakšid*	*kitašad*		*šutakšid*	
PARTICIPLE	*kāšidu*	*mukaššidu*	*mušakšidu*	*mukkašidu*	*muktašidu*	*muktaššidu*	*muštakšidu*	
INFINITIVE	*kašādu*	*kuššudu*	*šukšudu*	*nakšudu*	*kitašudu*	*kutaššudu*	*šutakšudu*	

§ 45. *Vocabulary.*

šapāru = to send
maḫaṣu = to smite
sapānu = to overcome
šalāmu = to prosper
zanānu = to send rain
tabāku = to pour out
tamāḫu = to hold

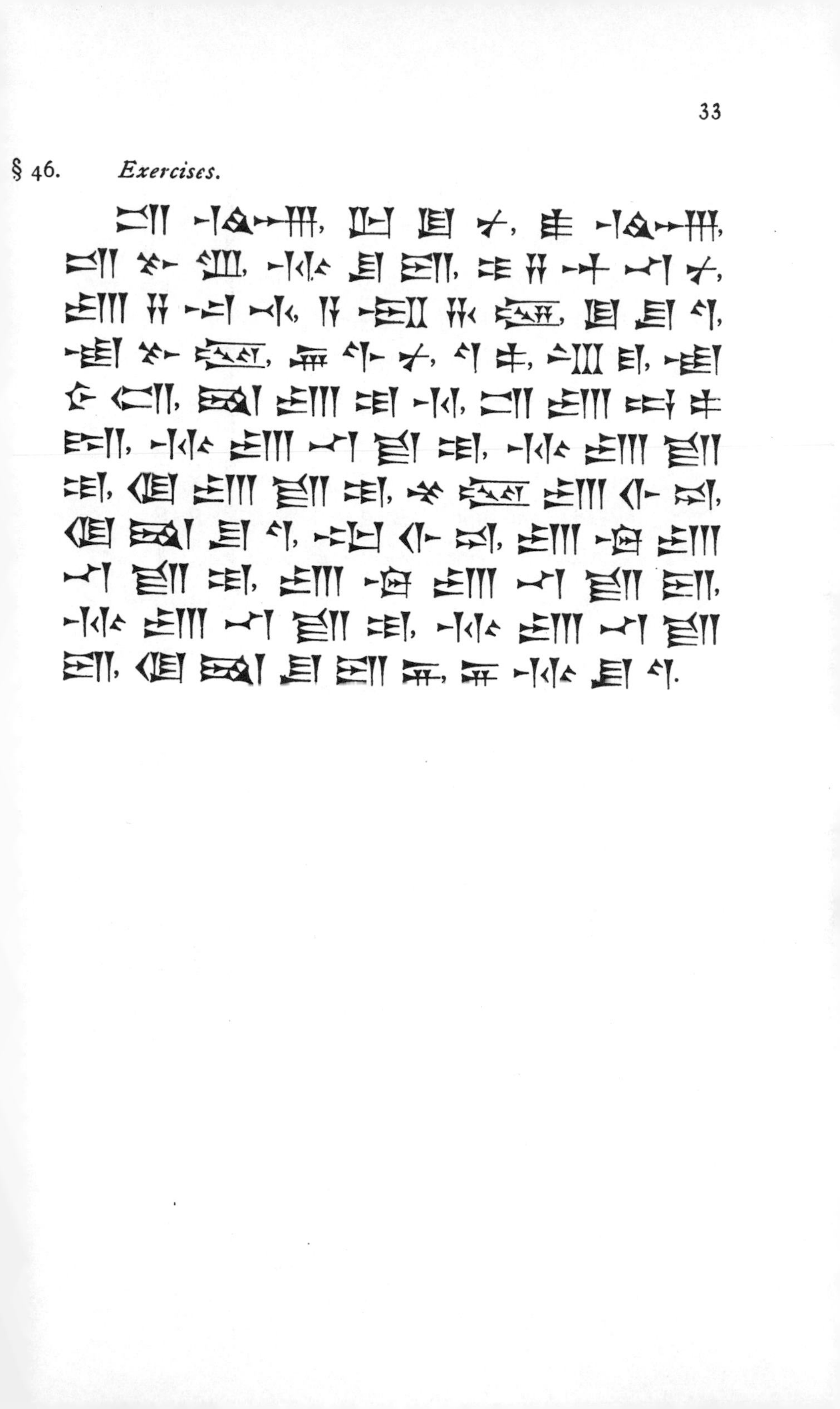

§ 46. *Exercises.*

CHAPTER XIII

§ 47. *Verbs with an initial n.*

	QAL	SHAFEL	NIFAL	IFTEAL	ISHTAFAL
PRESENT	*iddan*	*ušaddan*	*innadin*	*ittadan*	*uštaddan*
PRETERITE	*iddin*	*ušaddin*	*innadin*	*ittadin*	*uštaddin*
PERMANSIVE	*nadin*	*šuddun*	*naddun*	*tadin*	
IMPERATIVE	*idin*	*šuddin*	*naddin*		
PARTICIPLE	*nādinu*	*mušaddinu*	*munnadinu*	*muttadinu*	
INFINITIVE	*nadānu*	*šuddunu*	*naddunu*		

The remaining forms are comparatively regular.

§ 48. *Vocabulary.*

nadānu = to give *naṣāru* = to guard

§ 49. *Exercises.*

CHAPTER XIV

§ 50. *Verbs with a weak initial letter.*

	QAL	PAAL	SHAFEL	NIFAL	IFTEAL	IFTANEAL
PRESENT	*iḫḫaz*	*uḫḫaz*	*ušaḫḫaz*	*innaḫaz*	*ītaḫaz*	*ītanaḫaz*
	illak		*ušālak*		*ittalak*	*ittanalak*
	uššab	*uššab*	*ušāšab*	*i'ašab*	*ittašab*	*ittanašab*
	ettiḳ	*uttaḳ*	*ušētaḳ*	*innettiḳ*	*ētetiḳ*	*ētenetiḳ*
PRETERITE	*īḫuz*	*uḫḫiz*	*ušāḫiz*	*innaḫiz*	*ītaḫaz*	*ītanaḫaz*
	illik		*ušālik*		*ittalak*	*ittanalak*
	ūšib	*uššib*	*ušāšib*	*i'ašib*	*ittašab*	*ittanašab*
	ētiḳ	*uttiḳ*	*ušētiḳ*	*innettiḳ*	*ētetiḳ*	*ētenetiḳ*
PERMANSIVE	*aḫiz*	*uḫḫuz*	*šūḫuz*	*nāḫuz*	*ītaḫuz*	
	alik		*šūluk*		*italuk*	
	ašib	*uššub*	*šūšub*		*tašib*	
	etiḳ	*uttuḳ*	*šūtuḳ*	*nētuḳ*	*ētetuḳ*	
IMPERATIVE	*aḫuz*	*uḫḫiz*	*šuḫiz*	*nāḫiz*	*ītḫaz*	
	alik		*šūlik*		*itlak*	
	šib	*uššib*	*šūšib*		*tišab*	
	etiḳ	*uttiḳ*	*šūtiḳ*	*nētiḳ*	*ētetik*	

	QAL	PAAL	SHAFEL	NIFAL	IFTEAL	IFTANEAL
PARTICIPLE	*āḫizu*	*muḫḫizu*	*mušāḫizu*	*munnaḫizu*	*mūtaḫizu*	
	āliku		*mušāliku*		*muttaliku*	
	āšibu	*muššibu*	*mušāšibu*		*muttašibu*	
	ētiḳu	*muttiḳu*	*mušētiḳu*	*munnetiḳu*	*muttētiḳu*	
INFINITIVE	*aḫāzu*	*uḫḫuzu*	*šūḫuzu*	*nāḫuzu*	*ītaḫuzu*	
	alāku		*šūluku*		*italuku*	
	ašābu	*uššubu*	*šūšubu*		*itašubu*	
	etēḳu	*uttuḳu*	*šūtuḳu*	*ṇētuḳu*	*ētetuḳu*	

After studying carefully the above forms of verbs with a weak initial letter, the other forms of the same class of verbs will occasion no difficulty.

The verb ***aḫāzu*** begins with the equivalent of the Hebrew letter א, and is called initial א$_1$; ***alāku*** begins with the equivalent of ה, and is called initial א$_2$; ***ašābu*** with the equivalent of ו, and is called initial א$_6$; and ***etēḳu*** with the equivalent of ע, and is called initial א$_4$. There are verbs that begin with the equivalent of the Hebrew letters ח and י, and are called initial א$_3$ and initial א$_7$, respectively. Examples are, of the former, ***edēšu*** to be new, and of the latter, ***ešēru*** to be straight. Their forms will occasion no difficulty. The only other class of initial weak verbs is א$_5$, which begins with the equivalent of the Arabic غ. An example is ***erēbu*** to enter. This also will give no trouble.

§ 51. *Vocabulary.*

aḫāzu	= to hold	***alāku***	= to go
ašābu	= to dwell	***etēḳu***	= to march, go

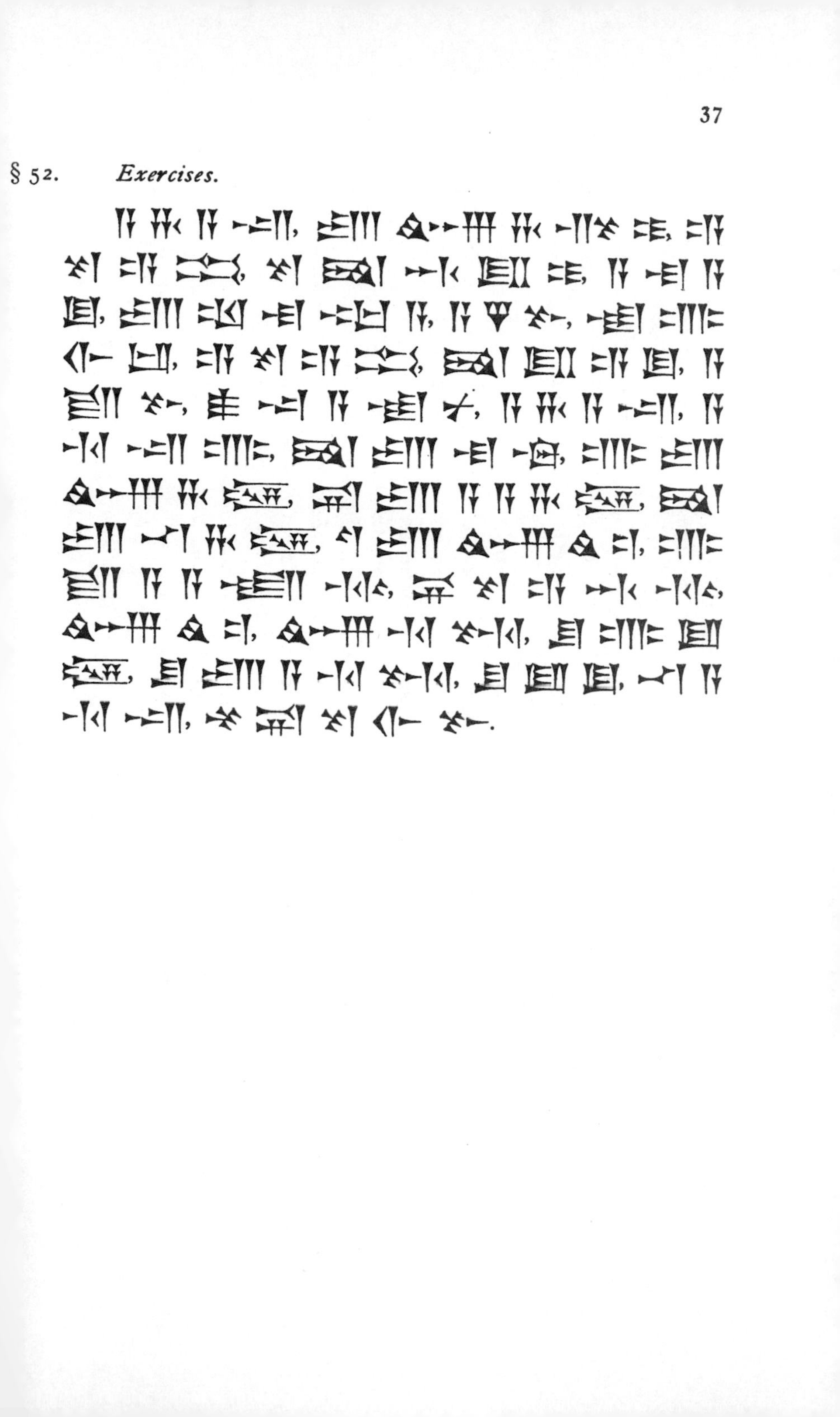

§ 52. *Exercises.*

[illegible]

CHAPTER XV

§ 53. *Verbs with a weak medial letter.*

	QAL	PAAL	NIFAL	IFTEAL	IFTAAL	IFTANEAL
PRESENT	*iša’al*			*išta’al*		*ištana’al*
	ikān	*ukān*	*ikkān*	*iktān*	*uktān*	*iktanunnu*
	iṭāb	*uṭāb*	*iṭṭāb*	*iṭṭāb*	*uṭṭāb*	
PRETERITE	*iš’al*			*išta’al*		*ištana’al*
	ikūn	*ukīn*	*ikkīn*	*iktūn*	*uktīn*	*iktanūn*
	iṭīb	*uṭīb*	*iṭṭīb*	*iṭṭīb*	*uṭṭīb*	
PERMANSIVE	*ša’il*			*šit’ul*		
	kēn	*kūn*		*kitūn*	*kutūn*	
	ṭāb	*ṭūb*				
IMPERATIVE	*ša’al*			*šit’al*		
	kūn	*kīn*		*kitān*	*kutīn*	
	ṭīb	*ṭīb*				
PARTICIPLE	*šā’ilu*			*mušta’ilu*		
	kā’inu,	*mukīnu*		*muktīnu*	*muktīnu*	
	ṭā’ibu	*muṭību*				
INFINITIVE	*ša’ālu*			*šit’ulu*		
	kānu	*kūnu*		*kitūnu*	*kutunnu*	
	ṭābu	*ṭūbu*				

The other forms of verbs with a weak medial are easily identified.

The verb *šaʾālu* has for a middle radical the equivalent of the Hebrew letter א, and is called medial א$_1$; *kānu* has for a middle radical the equivalent of the letter ו, and is called medial א$_6$; and *ṭābu* has for a middle radical the equivalent of י, and is called medial א$_7$. There are verbs which have for a middle radical the equivalent of the Hebrew letters ה, ח, ע, and of the Arabic letter غ. They are called medial א$_2$, א$_3$, א$_4$, and א$_5$, respectively. Examples of these are, *māru* to send, *rāmu* to love, *bēlu* to rule, and *baʾu* to seek. Their forms will occasion no difficulty.

§ 54. *Vocabulary.*

šaʾālu	= to ask	*kānu*	= to stand
ṭābu	= to be good	*maʾādu*	= to be many
mātu	= to die	*bēlu*	= to rule

§ 55. *Exercises.*

CHAPTER XVI

§ 56. *Verbs with a weak final letter.*

	QAL	PAAL	SHAFEL	NIFAL	IFTEAL	IFTANEAL
PRESENT	*ibani*	*ubanni*	*ušabni*	*ibbani*	*ibtani*	*ibtanani*
PRETERITE	*ibni*	*ubanni*	*ušabni*	*ibbani*	*ibtani*	*ibtanani*
PERMANSIVE	*bani*	*bunni*	*šubni*	*nabni*	*bitni*	
IMPERATIVE	*bini*	*bunni*	*šubni*	*nabni*	*bitani*	
PARTICIPLE	*bānū*	*mubannū*	*mušabnū*	*mubbanū*	*mubtanū*	
INFINITIVE	*banū*	*bunnū*	*šubnū*	*nabnū*	*bitnū*	

The remaining forms of this verb are easily identified.

The verb *banū* has for a final radical the equivalent of the Hebrew letter ה, which in these verbs really corresponds to the original ו and י, and is called final א$_{6,7}$. There are verbs which have for a final radical the equivalent of the Hebrew letters א, ה, ח, and ע. They are called final א$_1$, א$_2$, א$_3$, and א$_4$, respectively. Examples of these are, *malū* to fill, *nigū* to be light, *pitū* to open, and *šemū* to hear. Their forms will occasion no difficulty.

§ 57. *Vocabulary.*

banū = to build
manū = to count
maṣū = to find
pitū = to open
tibū = to come

§ 58. *Exercises.*

[illegible]

CHAPTER XVII

§ 59. ***Other irregular verbs.***

1. *Verbs with four radicals.*

	PAAL	SHAFEL	NIFAL	IFTAAL	ISHTAFAL
PRESENT	*uškalal*	*ušabalkat*	*ibbalakit*	*uštaḳlal*	*uštabalkat*
PRETERITE	*uškalil*	*ušabalkit*	*ibbalkit*	*uštaḳlil*	*uštabalkit*
PERMANSIVE	*šuḳalul*	*šubalkut*	*nabalkut*		*šutabalkut*
IMPERATIVE	*šuḳalil*	*šubalkit*	*nabalkit*		*šutabalkit*
PARTICIPLE	*muškalilu*	*mušbalkitu*	*mubbalkitu*		*muštabalkitu*
INFINITIVE	*šuḳalulu*	*šubalkutu*	*nabalkutu*		*šutabalkutu*

2. *Doubly weak verbs.*

Some verbs have two weak radicals. Such verbs exhibit the pecularities of both classes of weak verbs to which they belong. Thus the verb *idū* to know is both initial $\aleph_7$ and final $\aleph_4$.

3. *Verbs in which the second and third letters are the same.*

These are called *mediae geminatae*, and are in the main conjugated like the regular verb. In a few forms contraction of the second and third letters takes place. Thus *ša-lālu* to plunder, in the 3. m. s. perm. of the Qal has *šal* for *šalil.*

§ 60. *Vocabulary.*

šuḳalulu	= to swing	*balkatu*	= to tear down
idū	= to know	*šalālu*	= to plunder

§ 61. *Exercises.*

[illegible]

CHAPTER XVIII

§ 62. *The verb with suffixes.*

A verbal suffix may express: (1) the accusative, e. g., *al-ḳa-šú-nu-ú-ti*, I removed them; (2) the dative, e. g., *ad-din-šu*, I gave him; or (3) a prepositional phrase, e. g., *aš-bat-su*, she sits with him.

		Forms ending in Consonant with simple suffix	Forms ending in Consonant with augmented suffix	Forms in *ū*, *ā* with simple suffix	Forms in *ū*, *ā* with augmented suffix
Singular	3 m.	*iškunšū*	*iškunaššū*	*iškunūšū*	*iškunūniššu*
	3 f.	*iškunšī*	*iškunaššī*	*iškunūšī*	*iškunūniššī*
	2 m.	*iškunkā*	*iškunakkā*	*iškunūkā*	*iškunūnikkā*
	2 f.	*iškunkī*	*iškunakkī*	*iškunūkī*	*iškunūnikkī*
	1 c.	*iškunnī*	*iškunannī*	*iškunūnī*	*iškunū'inni*
Plural	3 m.	*iškunšunū*	*iškunaššunū*	*iškunūšunū*	*iškunūniššunū*
	3 f.	*iškunšinā*	*iškunaššinā*	*iškunūšinā*	*iškunūniššinā*
	2 m.	*iškunkunū*	*iškunakkunū*	*iškunūkunū*	*iškunūnikkunū*
	2 f.	*iškunkinā*	*iškunakkinā*	*iškunūkinā*	*iškunūnikkinā*
	1 c.	*iškunnā*	*iškunannā*	*iškunūnā*	*iškunū'innā*

		Forms in *ī* with simple suffix	Forms in *ī* with augmented suffix	Forms in *i*, *e* with simple suffix	Forms in *i*, *e* with augmented suffix
Singular	3 m.	*šuknīšū*	*šukniššū*	*ibnišū*	*ibnaššū*
	3 f.	*šuknīšī*	*šukniššī*	*ibnišī*	*ibnaššī*
	2 m.			*ibnikā*	*ibnakkā*
	2 f.			*ibnikī*	*ibnakkī*
	1 c.	*šuknīnī*	*šukninni*	*ibninī*	*ibnanni*
Plural	3 m.	*šuknīšunū*	*šukniššunū*	*ibnišunū*	*ibnaššunū*
	3 f.	*šuknišinā*	*šukniššinā*	*ibnišinā*	*ibnaššinā*
	2 m.			*ibnikunā*	*ibnakkunū*
	2 f.			*ibnikinā*	*ibnakkinā*
	1 c.	*šuknīnā*	*šukinnā*	*ibninā*	*ibnannā*

§ 63. *Exercises.*

CHAPTER XIX

THE NOUN

§ 64. *Formation of nouns.*

1. Some nouns are formed by merely adding vowels to the root consonants, e. g., ***šulmu***, peace, from ***šalāmu***, to be at peace.

2. Some nouns take a feminine termination, e. g., ***puluḫtu***, fear, from ***palāḫu***, to fear.

3. Some nouns are formed by the addition of prefixes. The prefix may be

(a) a vowel, e. g., ***ikribu***, prayer, from ***karābu***, to bless.

(b) *m* or *n*, e. g., ***mālaku***, way, from ***alāku***, to go; ***narāmu***, love, from ***rāmu***, to love.

(c) *š*, e. g., ***šurbū***, great, from ***rabū***, to be great.

(d) *t*, e. g., ***tamḫaru***, fight, from ***maḫāru***, to oppose.

4. A few nouns insert *t* after the first radical, e. g., ***ritpāšu***, wide, from ***rapāšu***, to be wide.

5. Some nouns have special terminations, chief of which are:

(a) ***ānu***, e. g., ***kurbānu***, offering, from ***karābu***, to pay homage to.

(b) *u*, e. g., ***maḫru***, former, from ***maḫāru***, to oppose.

(c) ***ūtu***, e. g., ***bēlūtu***, lordship, from ***bēlu***, lord. These are abstract nouns.

6. A few nouns drop the initial weak letter of the root, e. g., ***šubtu***, dwelling, from ***ašābu***, to dwell.

§ 65. *Exercises.* Determine the meaning of the following nouns from the glossary. In Assyrian dictionaries words are arranged not necessarily according to the consonants or vowels with which they happen to begin, but under their root. The root of a word is given in the form of the infinitive. For convenience, all nouns in this book are arranged in the glossary according to the consonants or vowels with which they begin. Verbs are arranged according to their infinitives.

The student's attention is called to the fact that *p* often changes place with *b*, *t* with *d*, *k* with *g* and *š* with *s*.

CHAPTER XX

§ 66. *Gender, number and case.*

1. Nouns have two genders, masculine and feminine. A few nouns are of common gender. Nouns of feminine gender are: (a) Most names of parts of the body; (b) Nouns that end in *tu*, *ti*, *ta* with or without one of the vowels, *a*, *e*, *i*, *u*, preceeding.

2. The plural of masculine nouns ends in *e* (or *i*), *āni*, *ā*, *ūti*; the plural of feminine nouns in *āti* (or *ēti*). Many nouns have more than one form of plural, e. g., *šadē* and *šadāni*, mountains.

3. The nominative case is usually marked by the ending *u*, the genitive by *i* and the accusative by *a*. There are many exceptions to the rule, the case endings being often employed indiscriminately.

4. The ending *u(m)* of a noun sometimes has the same force as a preposition, e. g., *bītum*, in the house, or with a following genitive, e. g., *ḳirbum Bābili* = *ina ḳirib B.*, in the midst of B. With suffixes the *m* is assimilated to the suffix, e. g.,

ḳatūa (for *ḳatū-ya*),	with my hand	
ḳātukka,	„ thy „	
ḳatuššu,	„ his „	etc.

§ 67. *Mimation.*

To nouns the particle *ma* or *m* is often appended. This is called *mimation*. It does not seem to affect the meaning or significance of the word to which it is attached.

§ 68. *Declension of a noun.*

	MASCULINE		FEMININE	
	Early form	Late form	Early form	Late form
Sing. nom.	*kalbum*	*kalbu*	*kalbatum*	*kalbatu*
gen.	*kalbim*	*kalbi*	*kalbatim*	*kalbati*
acc.	*kalbam*	*kalba*	*kalbatam*	*kalbata*
Plu. nom.	*kalbū*	*kalbānū/ī, kalbē*	*kalbātum*	*kalbātū/ī*
gen. acc.	*kalbī*	*kalbānī, kalbē*	*kalbātim*	*kalbātī*
Du. nom.	*kalbān*	*kalbān, kalbēn*	*kalbān*	*kalbān, kalbā/ē*
gen. acc.	*kalbēn*	*kalbā, kalbē*	*kalbēn*	*kalbān, kalbā/ē*

§ 69. *Vocabulary.*

kalbu	= dog	*šadū*	= mountain
girru	= expedition	*ilu*	= god
šulmu	= peace	*šumu*	= name
lišānu	= speech	*māru*	= son
libbu	= heart	*bēlu*	= lord
abu	= father	*amēlu*	= man

bēltu = lady
dimtu = tears
šarru = king
kalmatu = insect
mārtu = daughter
kibratu = region
maḫazu = city

§ 70. *Exercises.*

CHAPTER XXI

§ 71. *The construct state.*

1. When a noun stands by itself it is in the *absolute state*; when one noun, in the genitive, is joined to another it is in the *construct state.*

2. A noun in construct state, if it is singular, nom. or acc., generally drops the case-ending *u* or *a.* If the noun is in the genitive, the *i* of the genitive does not disappear. In some words a short vowel of the stem has already dropped out before the case-ending and this in the construct reappears, e. g., *zikru*, "mention", *zi-kir šu-mi-šu*, "mention of his name". The terminations, *āni*, *āti*, *ēti* and *ūti*, of plural nouns usually become *ān*, *āt*, *ēt* and *ūt.*

3. Another way of expressing the genitive relation

between two nouns is by the relative pronoun *ša*, e. g., *ilāni ša šamē.*

§ 72. *Apposition.*

When two substantives are in apposition it is not essential that they should agree in number. Thus, a noun in the singular sometimes stands in apposition to one in the plural, e. g., *alāni bīt šarru-ti*, "cities, royal dwellings". The same applies to participles used as nouns.

§ 73. *Construct of ilu and bēltu.*

		MASCULINE	FEMININE
Sing.	nom. gen. acc.	*il*	*bēlit*
Plu.	nom.	*ilū*	*bilāt*
	gen. acc.	*ilī*	*bilāt*
Du.	nom.	*ilā*	*biltā*
	gen. acc.	*ilē*	*biltē*

§ 74. *Vocabulary.*

ṭubbu	= joy	*kišādu*	= bank of a river
bābu	= gate	*apsū*	= ocean, abyss
šamū	= heaven	*irṣitu*	= earth
bītu	= house	*šalāṭu*	= to pierce

§ 75. *Exercises.*

CHAPTER XXII

§ 76. *Nouns with suffixes.*

		SINGULAR		PLURAL		
				nouns in *ū, ī, ē, ā*	nouns in *āni*	nouns in *ātu, āti, ētu, ēti*
Singular	3 m.	*māršū,*	*bēlitsū*	*mārūšū*	*šarrānišū*	*ḫiṭātēšū*
	3 f.	*māršā,*	*bēlitsā*	*mārūšā*	*šarrāniša*	*ḫiṭātēšā*
	2 m.	*mārkā,*	*bēlitkā*	*mārūkā*	*šarrānikā*	*ḫiṭātēkā*
	2 f.	*mārkī,*	*bēlitkī*	*mārūkī*	*šarrānikī*	*ḫiṭātēkī*
	1 c.	*mārī,*	*bēlitiiā*	*mārū'ā*	*šarrāniiā*	*ḫiṭātēiā*
Plural	3 m.	*māršunū,*	*bēlitsunū*	*mārūšunū*	*šarrānišunū*	*ḫiṭātēšunū*
	3 f.	*māršinā,*	*bēlitsinā*	*mārūšinā*	*šarrānišinā*	*ḫiṭātēšinā*
	2 m.	*mārkunū,*	*bēlitkunū*	*mārūkunū*	*šarrānikunū*	*ḫiṭātēkunū*
	2 f.	*mārkinā,*	*bēlitkinā*	*mārūkinā*	*šarrānikinā*	*ḫiṭātēkinā*
	1 c.	*mārnī,*	*bēlitnī*	*mārūnī*	*šarrāninī*	*ḫiṭātēnī*

Notice: In Genitive ***always*** *māri-* (instead of *mār*)!!

§ 77. *Vocabulary.*

ḫiṭītu = sin *idu* = hand, side

§ 78. *Exercises.*

CHAPTER XXIII

THE ADJECTIVE

§ 79. *Declension of Adjectives.*

Adjectives are declined in precisely the same way as nouns, and are of two genders, masculine and feminine. The masculine plural of adjectives is formed by means of the termination *ūti*, the feminine plural by the termination *āti*, or *ēti*, e. g., *gamru*, plu. *gamrūti*; *dannu*, plu. fem. *dannāti*; *limnu*, plu. fem. *limnēti*.

§ 80. *Comparison of Adjectives.*

1. The degree of comparison is usually expressed by an adjective with a long final vowel, e. g., *šaplū*, lower; *maḫrū*, former; *ēlēnū*, upper. Sometimes it is expressed by means of the preposition *ēli* or *ṣir*, over, e. g., *ṣir ša ābburti*, more than in the native place (lit., more over (that) of the native place).

2. The superlative is usually expressed by means of *ina*, in, among; or *ša*, of, e. g., *rabū ina* (or *ša*) *ilāni*, the greatest of the gods.

§ 81. *Vocabulary.*

gamru = complete		*dannu* = strong	
limnu = evil		*rabū* = great	
damḳu = favourable		*šaplū* = lower	
maḫrū = former		*ēlēnū* = upper	

§ 82. *Exercises.*

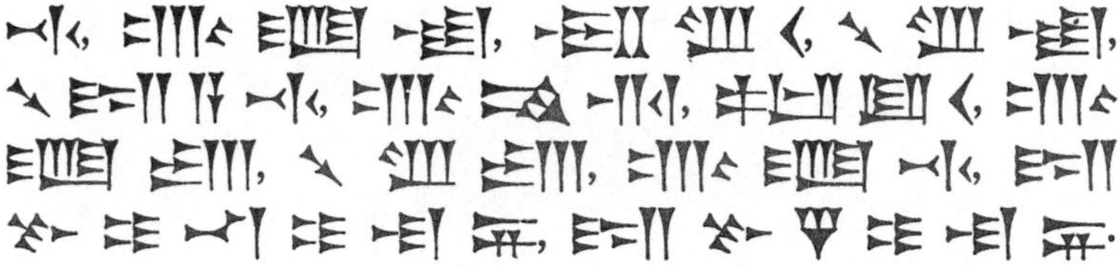

CHAPTER XXIV

NUMERALS

§ 83. *Cardinals.*

NUMBER	SIGN	PRONUNCIATION
1	𒁹	*išten*
2	𒈫	*šina*
3	𒐈	*šalašu*
4	𒐉	*arbaʾu*
5	𒐊	*ḫamšu*
6	𒐋	*šiššu*
7	𒐌	*siba*
8	𒐍	*samānu*
9	𒐎	*tišu*
10	𒌋	*ešru*
11	𒌋𒁹	*išten-ešru*
12	𒌋𒈫	*šina-ešru*
20	𒎙	*ešrā*
30	𒌍	*šalāšā*
40	𒐏	*irbā*
50	𒐐	*ḫanšā*
60	𒁹	*šuššu*
70	𒁹𒌋	*sibā*

NUMBER	SIGN	PRONUNCIATION
80		*samanā*
90		*tišā*
100		*me*
200		*šina-me*
600		*ner*
1000		*līmu* (orig. *li'mu*)
2000		*šina-līmu*
3600		*šar*

In the sexagesimal system is the mathematical unit; in the decimal system it is . Thus, by the sexagesimal system, 1921 would be , and by the decimal system, .

§ 84. *Ordinals.*

The ordinals are formed by using the cardinals with , *kam*, following, e. g., , *maḫrū*, first. Second is *šanū*; third, *šalšu*; and fourth, *rebū*. The others were usually pronounced like the ordinals.

§ 85. *Fractions.*

NUMBER	SIGN	PRONUNCIATION
$\frac{1}{2}$		*mišlu*
$\frac{1}{3}$		*šuššānu*
$\frac{2}{3}$		*šinipu*
$\frac{5}{6}$		*parap*

§ 86. *Distributives.*

These are formed either by adding *-šu* or *-anu*, e. g., *šiten-šu*, twice, or *šanianu*. In earlier texts the word for "time" is *ādu*, e. g., *ādi šina*, times two = twice. "Both" is expressed by *killallēn*, e. g., *killallē-šunu*, both of them.

§ 87. *Exercises.*

CHAPTER XXV

ADVERBS

§ 88. *Adverbs of manner.*

ki-a-am, so, thus, e. g., *šarru ki-a-am i-ḳab-bi*, thus saith the king.

mā, *umma*, thus, as follows, e. g., *ṭi-e-mu ut-te-ru-ni ma-a*, they brought me news as follows.

§ 89. *Adverbs of time.*

adū, now, e. g., *a-du-u u-mu-us-su u-sal-la*, now daily do I pray.

Other adverbs of time are: *umā*, now; *eninnu*, now (opposed to "formerly"); *matīma*, *matema*, whensoever, at any time; with negative, never.

90. *Interrogative adverbs.*

mēnu, *mīnu*, *mīni*, how? e. g., *a-na-ku-ma mi-i-nu a-ḳab-bi*, how shall I speak?

Other interrogatives are: *ana mēni, ammēni, ammīni,* why?; *adi mati,* how long?

§ 91. *Negative and prohibitive adverbs.*

lā, ul, not, e. g., *ša la ik-nu-šu a-na ni-ri-ia,* who had not submitted to my yoke; *ul a-kul,* I have not eaten.

lā, in prohibitions, is followed by the present, e. g., *la tal-lak,* do not go.

ai, not, particle of prohibition, is followed by the preterite.

ē, not, particle of prohibition, is used with the second person singular of the preterite.

§ 92. *Adverbs of emphasis.*

lū, verily, is placed before the third person masc. sing. and plu., and the first person, sing. and plu. of the preterite. It usually emphasises the verb, but not always, e. g., *al-lik* and *lu-u al-lik,* I went. When the verb begins with the vowel *u, lū* may combine with it to form a single word, e. g., *a-šar-šu-nu lu-maš-še-ru* (for *lū umašširū*), their place they deserted.

lū, as a precative particle is employed with the preterite and the permansive to express a wish; e. g., 3. s. *liškun,* 1. s. *luškun.*

ī, come!, cohortative particle, is used with the first person plural of the preterite.

ē, ī, up!, cohortative particle, is used with the second person singular of the imperative.

§ 93. *Adverbs appended enclitically.*

ma is appended for emphasis to pronouns, nouns, verbs and adverbs, e. g., *at-ta-ma kīma* *[ilu]Šamaš,* since thou art like Šamaš.

mi is appended for emphasis to verbs, especially in relative clauses.

ū is appended as an interrogative particle.

§ 94. *The adverbial ending iš.*

The ending *iš* or *eš* is very common, e. g.. *rabīš*, greatly; *eliš*, above; *šapliš*, below; *šalmeš*, peacefully; *umišamma*, daily (*iš* with reduplicated *ma* for strengthening).

The ending *āniš* means in many cases "like", e. g., *abūbāniš*, storm-like, flood-like.

§ 95. *Vocabulary.*

ḳabū, *ḳibū*	= to speak	*ṭēmu*	= understanding, news
umussu	= daily	*salū*	= to pray
kanāšu	= to submit	*nīru*	= yoke
akālu	= to eat	*alāku*	= to go
šiptu	= incantation	*marṣu*	= sick
ṭeḫū	= to draw near	*ašru*	= place
mašāru	= to leave	*epēšu*	= to do, make
šašmu	= battle	*ana*	= to
arādu	= to go down	*kištu*	= wood
mārtu	= daughter		

§ 96. *Exercises.*

CHAPTER XXVI

PREPOSITIONS

§ 97. In Assyrian prepositions are sometimes written phonetically and sometimes ideographically. The following are the principal prepositions, together with their ideograms and the forms they most commonly assume when written phonetically.

PREPOSITION	IDEO-GRAPHICALLY	PHONETICALLY	MEANING
ina	𒀸	𒄿 𒈾	in
ana	𒁹	𒀀 𒈾	to
ištu	𒋫	𒅖 𒌅	from
ultu	𒋫	𒌌 𒌅	from
itti	𒆠	𒀉 𒋾	with
eli	𒌋𒅗	𒂊 𒇷	on, upon
ṣīr	𒂔	𒍢 𒅕	on, against
adi	𒂗	𒀀 𒁲	up to, to, together with
gādu		𒂵 𒁺	up to, to, together with
arki	𒂕	𒅈 𒆠	after, behind
balū		𒁀 𒇻	without
kī		𒆠 𒄿	like, as
kīma	𒁶	𒆠 𒈠	like
aššu(m), orig. *ana šum*		𒀾 𒋗	concerning, because of
kūm		𒆪 𒌝	instead of
kirib		𒆠 𒆕	in, within
libbi	𒊮	𒇸 𒁉	in, within
pāni	𒅆	𒉺 𒉌	before

PRE-POSITION	IDEO-GRAPHICALLY	PHONETICALLY	MEANING
maḫar			before
ḳabal			in the midst of
ḳabalti			in the midst of
bīrit			between
pūt			opposite

§ 98. There are compound prepositions:

ina muḫḫi		on, concerning, against
ana muḫḫi		on, concerning, against
ina bīri		between
ana tarṣi		against
ina tarṣi		opposite
ištu tarṣi		from, since.

§ 99. There are other compound prepositions, such as: *ina eli*, *ana eli*, upon; *ina kirib*, *ina kirbi*, in; etc.

CHAPTER XXVII

CONJUNCTIONS

100. The following is a list of the principal Assyrian conjunctions:

u = and (connecting words as well as sentences)

ma = and (connecting two verbs; appended to the first)

enuma, *inuma*, *inu*, *inum* = when

kī, *kī ša* = as, when

akī ša = as

adi = while, so long as, till, until

ištu, *ultu* = since

arki ša = after

šumma = if

aššu ša } = because
aššu }

lū }
ū } = or
ū lū }

lū .... lū = either .... or
= whether .... or

lū .... ū = either .... or
= whether .... or

lū .... ū lū = either .... or
= whether .... or

§ 101. *Vocabulary.*

bašū	= to be	*banū*	= to make
pitū	= to open	*bābu*	= gate
amātu	= word	*naṣāru*	= to keep
nakaru	= foe	*aḫū*	= hostile
mama	= any	*šanū*	= other
māru	= son	*mārtu*	= daughter

§ 102. *Exercises.*

SYNTAX

CHAPTER XXVIII

103. *The noun.*

1. Nouns are found in three states, emphatic, absolute, and construct.

(1) The emphatic state is marked by a suffixed vowel, e. g., *šarru*, king.

(2) The absolute and construct are illustrated in §§ 64—75.

2. The accusative, as well as indicating the object, expresses the direction towards which, e. g., *Aššur*, to Assyria; it also expresses time, e. g., *um 13 kan*, on the thirteenth day.

3. A double accusative follows such verbs as *epēšu*, *nadānu*, etc.

4. The genitive relationship is expressed by:

(1) the construct state of the first of two nouns, e. g., *šar šarrāni*, king of kings,

(2) *ša*, e. g., *šangu ša Bēl*, priest of Bel,

(3) *ša* and a pronominal suffix, e. g., *alānišu ša Aššur^{ki}*, the cities of Assyria.

5. Two nouns may stand in apposition, e. g., *zunnu nuḫšu*, rain, flood.

04. *The adjective.*

1. The words *kalū*, *gimru*, *gimirtu*, with a suffix to express "all", stand in apposition to their nouns, e. g., *mātāti kalīšina*, the lands, their totality; *ilāni gimrašun*, all gods.

2. The word *gabbu*, all, follows its noun without a suffix, e. g., *mātāti gabbu*, all lands.

3. The adjective regularly follows its noun, e. g., *šarru dannu*, the mighty king.

4. If the noun has a suffix and is qualified by an adjective, the suffix comes between the noun and the adjective, e. g., *mulmullēia zaḳtūti*, my sharp arrows.

5. When an adjective qualifies more than one noun, it comes after the last, e. g., *mātāti u ḫuršāni dannūti*, the mighty lands and mountains.

6. An adjective with a collective noun may be in the singular or plural, e. g., *iṣṣūr šamē muttaprišu*, or *muttaprišūti*, the winged birds of heaven.

7. An adjective with a gentilic noun is put in the plural, e. g., *Madāia rūḳūti*, the district Medes.

§ 105. *Numerals.*

1. The cardinal numerals, 3—10, are either placed before their nouns (in genitive), or after them in apposition, e. g., *sibitti ūmī*, seven days; *šar kibrātim arba'im*, king of the four quarters.

2. Usually the noun with a number above 10 is placed in the singular, e. g., 10 000 *arītu*, 10 000 shields.

3. The distributive numeral is formed by means of the cardinal with the suffix *-šu*, e. g., *šinišu*, twice.

4. Ordinal numerals are treated as adjectives, e. g., *ina šatti šalulti*, in the third year.

§ 106. *Vocabulary.*

mētiḳu	=	course	*girru*	=	expedition
sisū	=	horse	*epištu*	=	deed
ṭābu	=	good	*ašru*	=	place
rūḳu	=	distant	*šemū*	=	to hear
tukultu	=	help			

§ 107. *Exercises.*

CHAPTER XXIX

108. *Verbal nouns.*

1. The participle takes its object in the genitive, e. g., *ēmid šarrāni*, the subduer of kings.

2. The infinitive is used as a noun, e. g., *nadān ilāni*, restoration of the gods; or as a verb, e. g., *šuttu pašāru*, to interpret a dream.

109. *The finite verb.*

1. An independent pronoun may replace a verbal suffix, e. g., *ušannā ia-a-ti*, he told it to me.

2. A noun in the indirect object is introduced by *ana*, e. g., *ana ga-ti-ia umallū*, he entrusted to me.

3. Some verbs govern two accusatives, e. g., *šaḳū*, to give some one to drink, etc.

110. *Vocabulary.*

šēpu	= foot	*ṣabātu*	= to set forth
kanāšu	= to prostrate	*nazāzu*	= to take up
ummānu	= troops	*narāru*	= help
ezēbu	= to save	*biltu*	= present
mandattu	= gift		

§ 111. *Exercises.*

CHAPTER XXX

§ 112. *The Simple Sentence.*

1. *Declaratory sentences* are common, e. g., *ilu damḳu*, god is gracious.

(1) The gender and number of the predicate are determined by the gender and number of the subject. There are, however, many exceptions.

(2) The object of a transitive verb may precede or follow it.

2. *Negative declaratory sentences* take the particle *lā*, e. g., *emūḳ lā nībi*, a countless army; *ul* is also used, e. g., *ul išemmū*, they hear not.

3. *Prohibitive sentences* are expressed, (1) by *lā*, e. g., *lā tasakip*, cast not down; (2) by *lu lā*, e. g., *šarru lu lā i-pa-laḫ*, let the king fear not at all; (3) by *a-a*, e. g., *ki-bi-ra a-a irši*, burial shall he not receive; (4) by *ē*, e. g., *ē tassaḫrī*, do not turn around.

4. *Optative and cohortative sentences* are expressed, (1) by *lū*, e. g., *lū balṭātā*, mayest thou be well; *li-ib-lu-uṭ* (for *lū iblut*), let him live; (2) by *ī* (*ē*), e. g., *i ni-pu-uš šašma*, let us fight with each other.

5. *Emphatic sentences* are expressed by *lū*, e. g., *lū allik*, I certainly went.

6. *Interrogative sentences* are expressed by an enclitic *ū*, e. g., *i-zir-tu-ū ina libbi šaṭrat*, is a curse written thereon? The negative is *ul*, e. g., *ul a-na-ku-ū*, am I not.

7. *Relative clauses* are usually introduced by *ša*, the verb ending in a vowel, e. g., *ša itbalu*, who had carried off. Sometimes the *ša* is omitted, e. g., *bītu ēpušu*, the house which I built.

8. *Conjunctional relative clauses* are introduced by a conjunction (or preposition), the verb ending in a vowel, e. g., *ultu ēmedu mātašu*, after I had subdued his land.

9. *Conditional clauses* are usually introduced by the particle *šumma*, e. g., *šumma aššata mussu izīrma*, if a wife takes a dislike towards her husband. But the particle may be omitted, e. g., *šarru ana dīni lā īgul*, should the king not obey the laws.

113. *The Compound Sentence.*

1. *Copulative sentences* are often placed side by side without any connecting particle. But when they are joined by a copula, the particle is *u* in nominal sentences, and *ma* in verbal sentences, e. g., *šunu liḳtūma anāku lum'id*, let them perish, but let me increase.

2. *Circumstantial clauses* are expressed by the present, the principal verb having an enclitic *ma*, e. g., *innabitma ibaḳam ziḳnāšu*, he fled, tearing his beard.

14. *Vocabulary.*

balāṭu	= to live	*šakānu*	= to set
šapāru	= to send	*magāru*	= to be favourable
maḳātu	= to fall, to overthrow	*ištaritum*	= a goddess
pašāru	= to annul	*ṭaḫū*	= to approach
ḳibītu	= command	*mašū*	= to forget
amēlu	= man	*ardu*	= slave
agāru	= to hire	*mātu*	= to die
epištu	= deed	*šīru*	= flesh (heart)

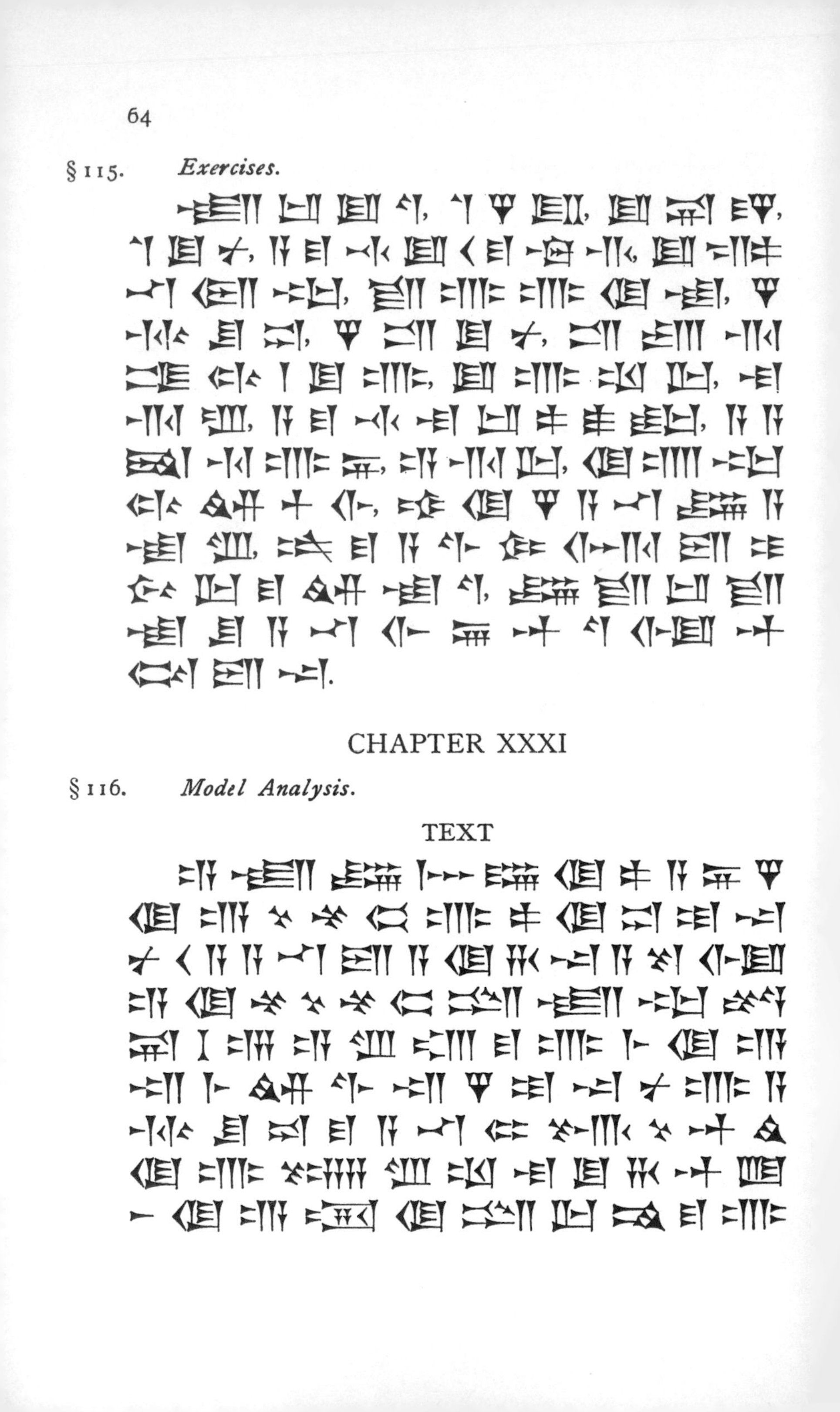

§ 115. *Exercises.*

CHAPTER XXXI

§ 116. *Model Analysis.*

TEXT

TRANSLITERATION

e-li šarrāni ^{amēlu}*ki-pa-a-ni ša ki-rib* ^{mātu}*Mu-ṣur u-pa-ki-du abu ba-nu-u-a a-na da-a-ki ḫa-ba-a-te u e-ki-mu* ^{mātu}*Mu-ṣur il-li-ka ṣīr-uš-šu-un e-ru-um-ma u-šib ki-rib* ^{alu}*Me-im-pi alu ša abu ba-nu-u-a ik-šú-du-ma a-na mi-ṣir* ^{mātu} ^{ilu}*Ašur*^{ki} *u-tir-ru al-la-ku ḫa-an-ṭu ina ki-rib Ninā*^{ki} *il-lik-am-ma u-ša-an-na-a ia-a-ti eli ip-še-e-ti an-na-a-ti lib-bi i-gu-ug-ma iṣ-ṣa-ru-uḫ ka-bit-ti áš-ši ḳātā*^{II}*-ia u-sal-li* ^{ilu}*Ašur u* ^{ilu}*Ištar Aššur-i-tu ad-ki-e e-mu-ki-ia ṣi-ra-a-te ša* ^{ilu}*Ašur u* ^{ilu}*Ištar u-mal-lu-u kātu*^{II}*-u-a a-na* ^{mātu}*Mu-ṣur u* ^{mātu}*Ku-u-si uš-te-eš-še-ra ḫar-ra-nu.*

TRANSLATION

Against the kings (and) governors, whom in Egypt, the father who begat me had installed, to slay, to plunder and to seize Egypt he marched. Against them he went in and settled himself in Memphis, a city which the father who begat me had conquered, and to the border of Assyria had annexed. A swift messenger into Nineveh came, and informed me concerning these matters. My heart was wroth and stirred was my spirit. I raised my hands; I prayed unto Ašur and Ištar of Assyria; I summoned my supreme forces, which Ašur and Ištar had filled in my hands, (and) to Egypt and Ethiopia I directed the way.

ANALYSIS

eli preposition, against, on, upon, concerning.

šarrāni noun, plu. masc. of *šarru*, king, gov. by *eli*.

amēlu determinative for male persons.

kipāni noun, plu. masc. of *ḳipū*, governor, gov. by *eli*.

ša rel. pron. referring to *šarrāni* and *kipāni*.

kirib preposition, in, within.

mātu determinative for countries.

Muṣur Egypt.

upakidu third masc. sing. Pret. Paal, variant of *upakkid*, from the verb *paḳādu*, to entrust, II, to install.

abu father.

banūa participle Qal, from the verb *banū*, to create, to beget, with first per. sing. suff., my begetter.

ana preposition, to.

dāki infinitive, governed by *ana*, from the verb *dāku*, to slay.

ḫabāte infinitive, governed by *ana*, from the verb *ḫabātu*, to plunder.

u conjunction.

ekīmu (for *ekēmu*) infinitive, governed by *ana*, from the verb *ekēmu*, to seize.

illika third masc. sing. Pret. Qal, with overhanging *a* (see p. 68) from the verb *alāku*, to go, to march. The subject of the verb is really *abu*.

ṣīruššūn preposition *ṣīr*, on, upon, against, phonetic *uš*, pron. suffix *šūn*, them, for *ana ṣiri-šun*, see § 66, 4.

erūmma variant for *erūb + ma*. Third masc. sing. Pret. Qal, from the verb *erēbu*, to go; with the conjunction *ma*. The subject is *abu*.

ušib third masc. sing. Pret. Qal from the verb *ašābu*, to dwell, to settle. The subject is *abu*.

alu is determinative for cities. The next *alu* is an ideogram, meaning city.

ikšuduma third masc. sing. Pret. Qal from the verb *kašādu*, to conquer. The subject is *abu*. *ma* is a conjunction.

miṣir construct of the noun *miṣru*, border. It is dependent upon the following noun *mātu*.

ilu Ašur is the Assyrian name of Assyria, meaning, with *mātu*, the "land of the god Ašur".

ki is a determinative suffixed to names of places.

utīrru third masc. sing. Pret. Paal from the verb *tāru*, to turn, II_1 to annex.

allaku noun in the absolute, messenger.

ḫanṭu adjective following its noun, swift, originally *ḫamṭu*.

ina kirib compound preposition, into.

illikamma, see above; the first *m* is a phonetic complement.

ušānnā third masc. sing. Pret. Paal from the verb *šanū*, to repeat, II_1 to inform.

iāti accusative of the pers. pron. first pers. sing.

ipšēti plu. of the noun *ipištu*, matter, thing.

annāti fem. plu. of the dem. pron. *annū*, this.

libbi noun from *libbu*, heart, with pron. suff. of first pers. sing.

igūgma third masc. sing. Pret. Qal from the verb *agāgu*, to be angry.

iṣṣaruḫ third masc. sing. Pret. Nifal from the verb *ṣarāḫu*, to cry aloud, IV_1 to be stirred.

kabitti noun sing. with first pers. pron. suffix, from the noun *kabittu*, spirit.

ašši first sing. Pret. Qal from the verb *našū*, to left up.

kātā II-ia noun dual with first pers. pron. suffix; from the noun *ḳātu*, hand.

usalli first sing. Pret. Paal from the verb *salū*, II_1 to pray to.

Aššurītu, the ending *itu* indicates a gentilic noun.

adkē first sing. Pret. Qal from the verb *dikū*, to summon.

emukia noun plu. from *emūḳu*, might, with first pers. pron. suffix.

ṣirāte adjective plu., following its noun, from *ṣīru*, high, supreme.

umallū third masc. plu. Pret. Paal from the verb *malū*, to fill.

uštēššera first sing. Pret. Ishtafal from the verb *ešēru*, III_2 to direct (the way). The final *a* is an example of the way in which all forms of the verb which end in a consonant may take one of the three short vowels *a*, *i*, or *u* as an overhanging letter; [but originally the forms ending in *a* are the modus of continuation (*-ā* from *-an*, comp. *illikam-ma* for *illikan-ma*). F. H.]

ḳatūa "in my hand", see § 66, 4; for *ana ḳatīa*.

ḫarrānu noun, direct object of the preceeding verb, meaning way.

This text is taken from Asurbanipal's Rassam-Cylinder, I, 57—68; repeated in p. 71 f.

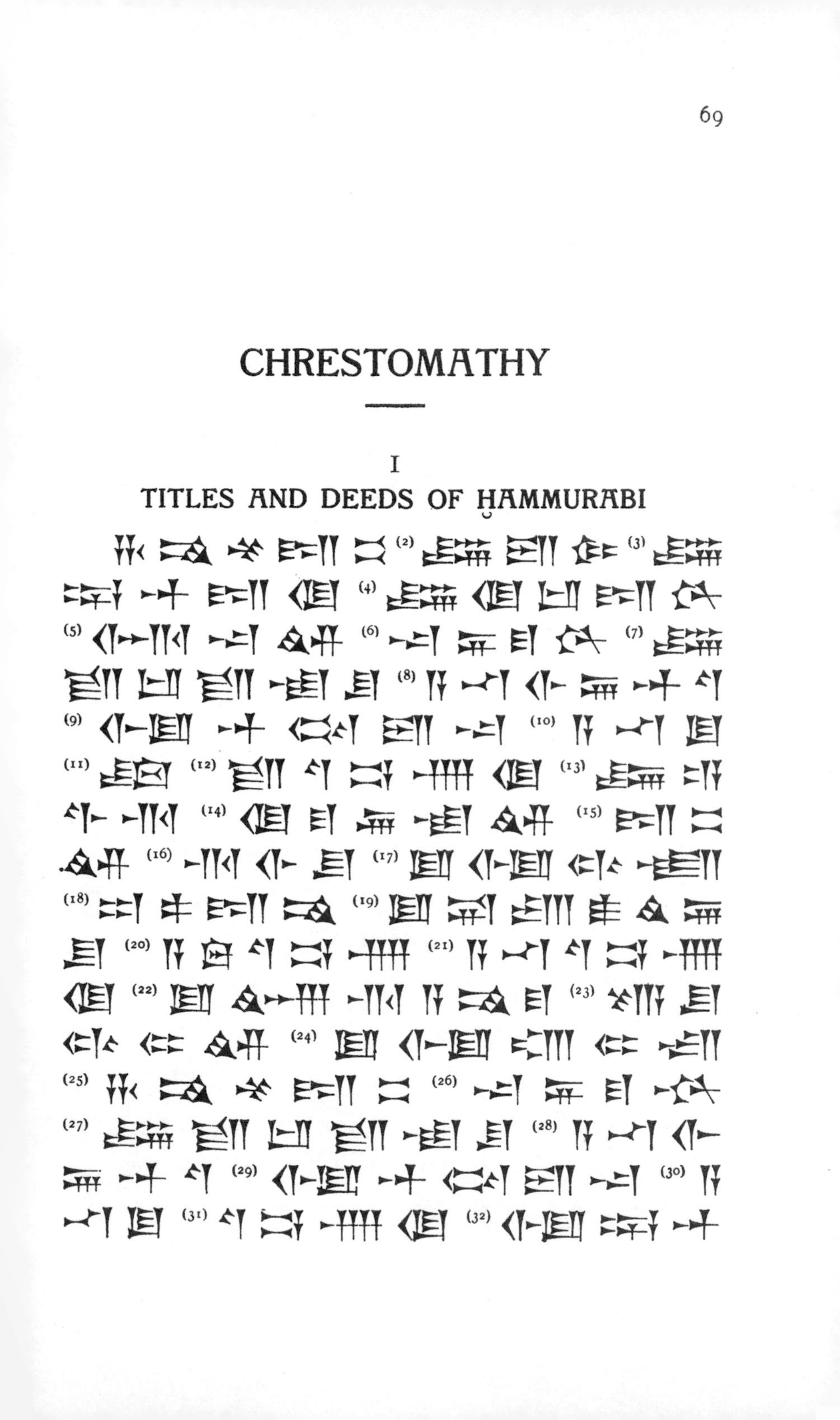

CHRESTOMATHY

I

TITLES AND DEEDS OF ḪAMMURABI

(Br. Mus., No. 12215 and comp. L. W. KING, The Letters and Inscriptions of Hammurabi, III, p. 177—179; line 42 is to be transcribed *šarru in šàr-rí* "a king for the kings", var. *šarru in šarrī-šú*).

II

THE SIEGE OF DAMASCUS AND THE TRIBUTE OF JEHU

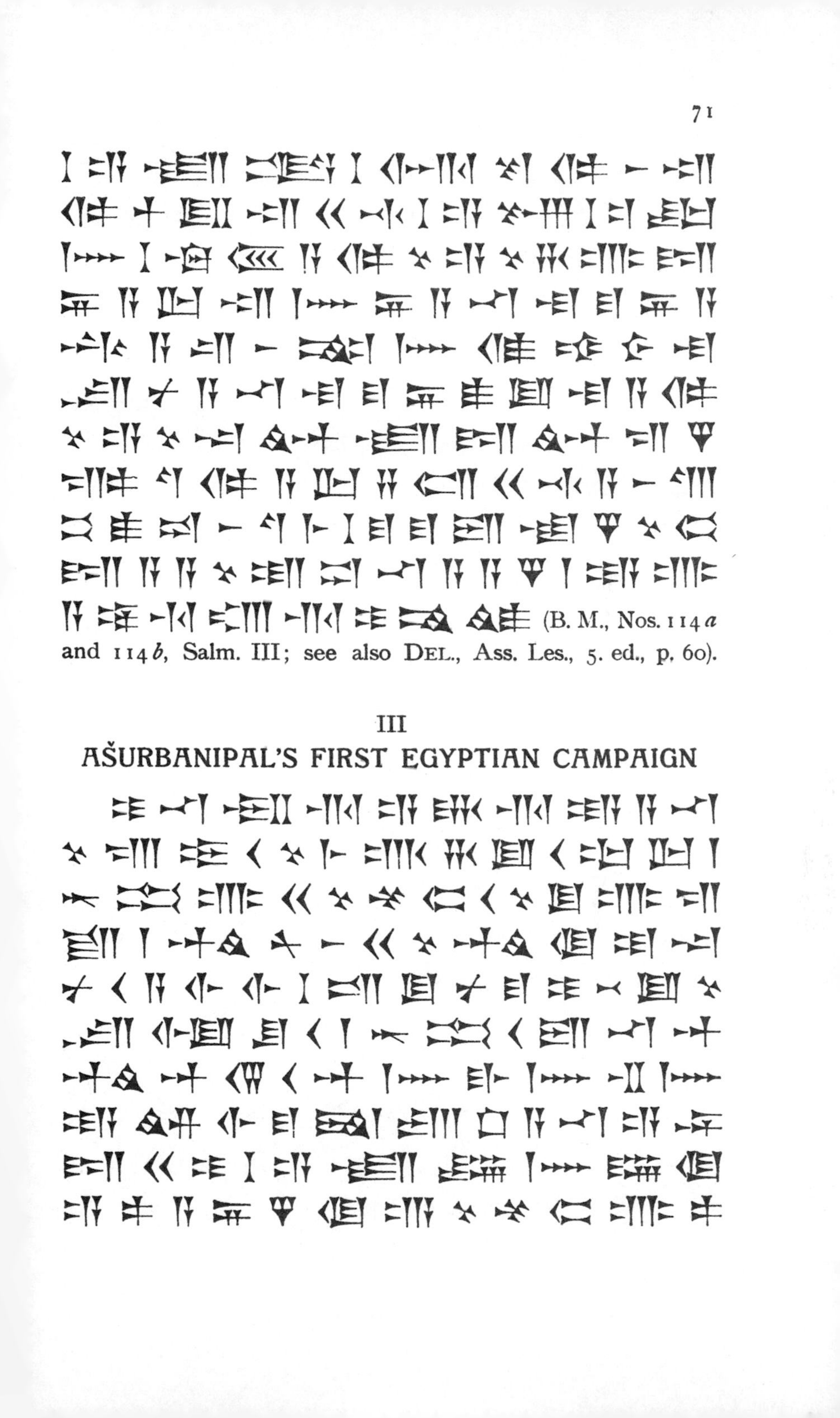

(B. M., Nos. 114*a* and 114*b*, Salm. III; see also DEL., Ass. Les., 5. ed., p. 60).

III

AŠURBANIPAL'S FIRST EGYPTIAN CAMPAIGN

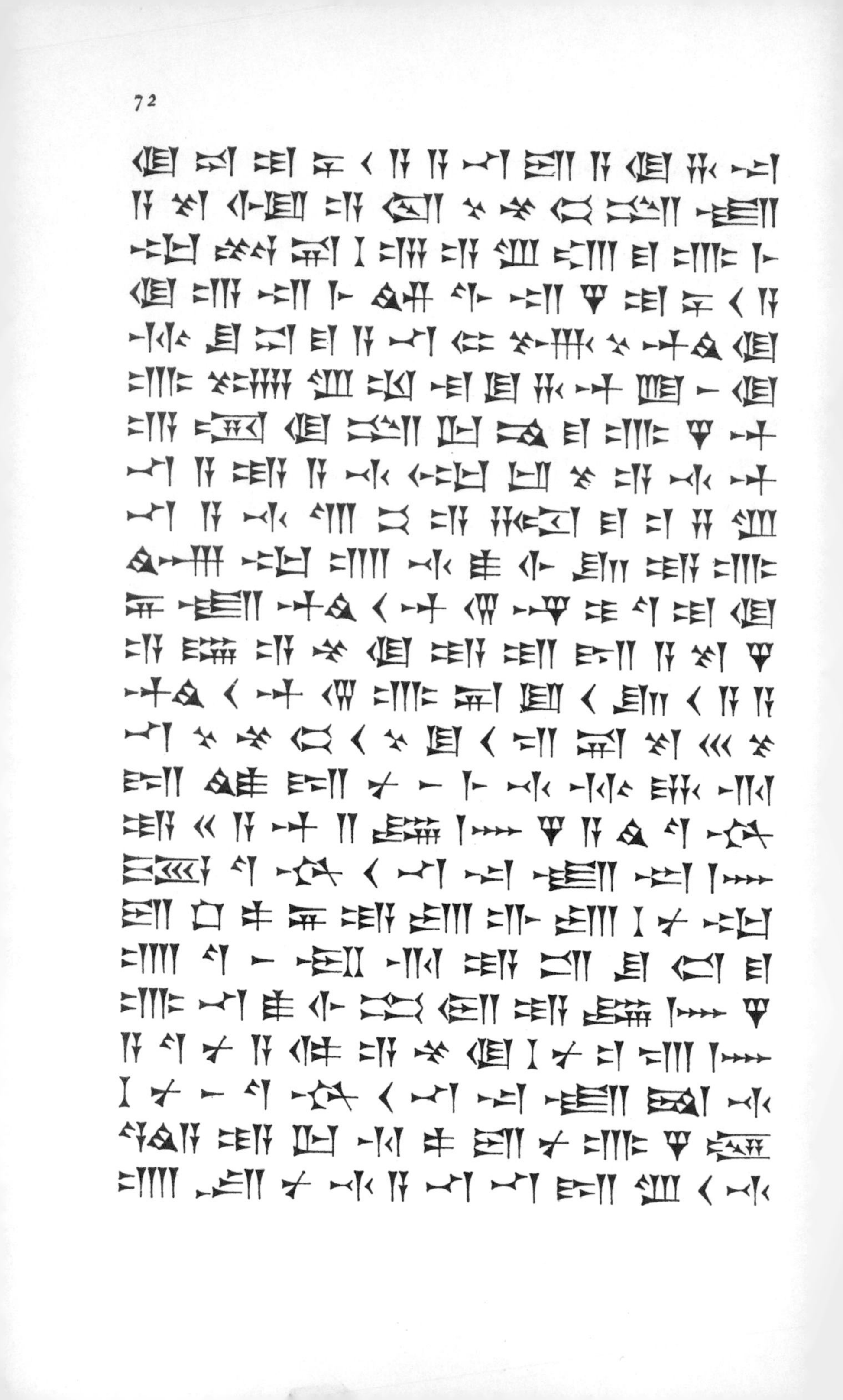

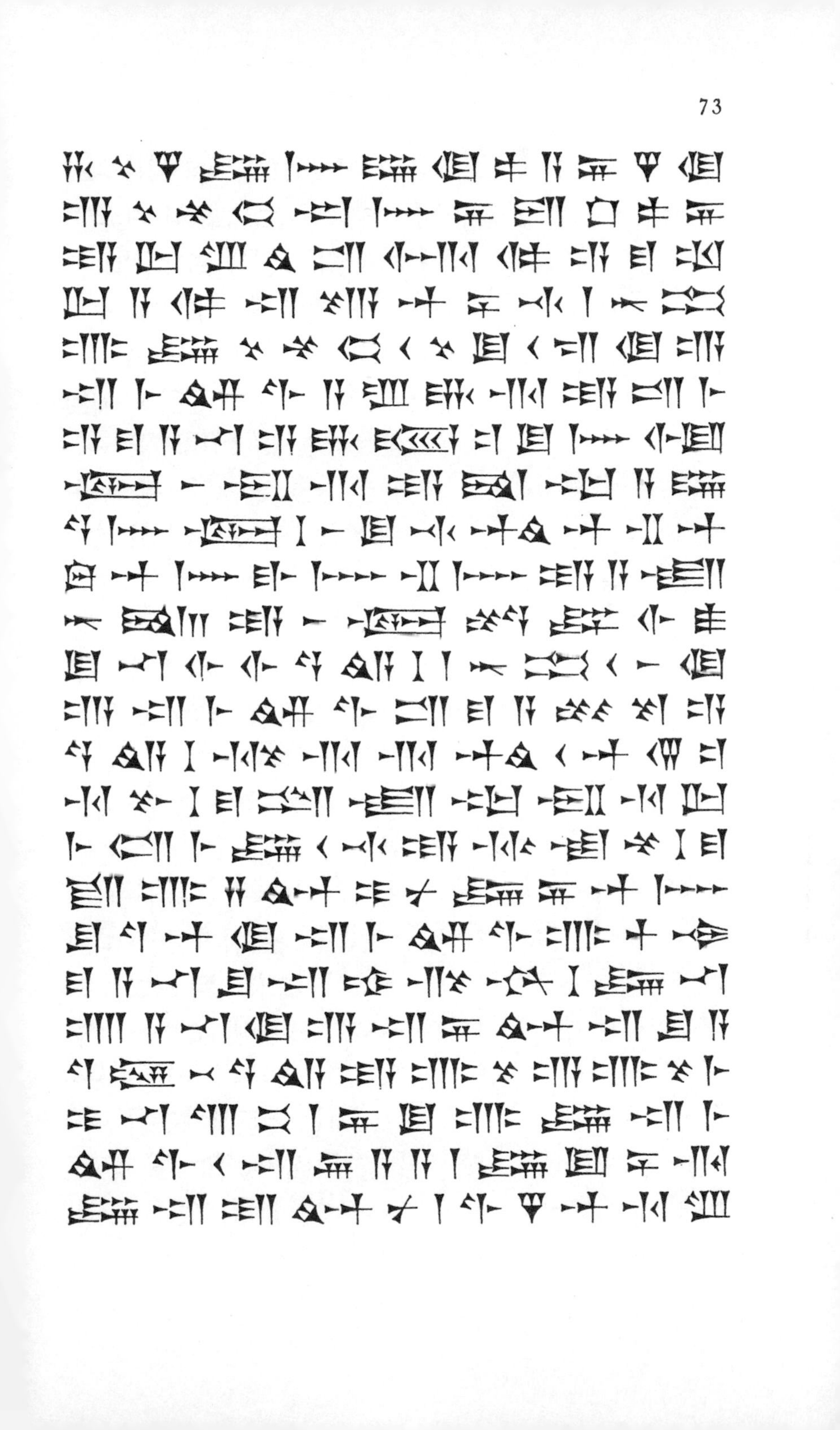

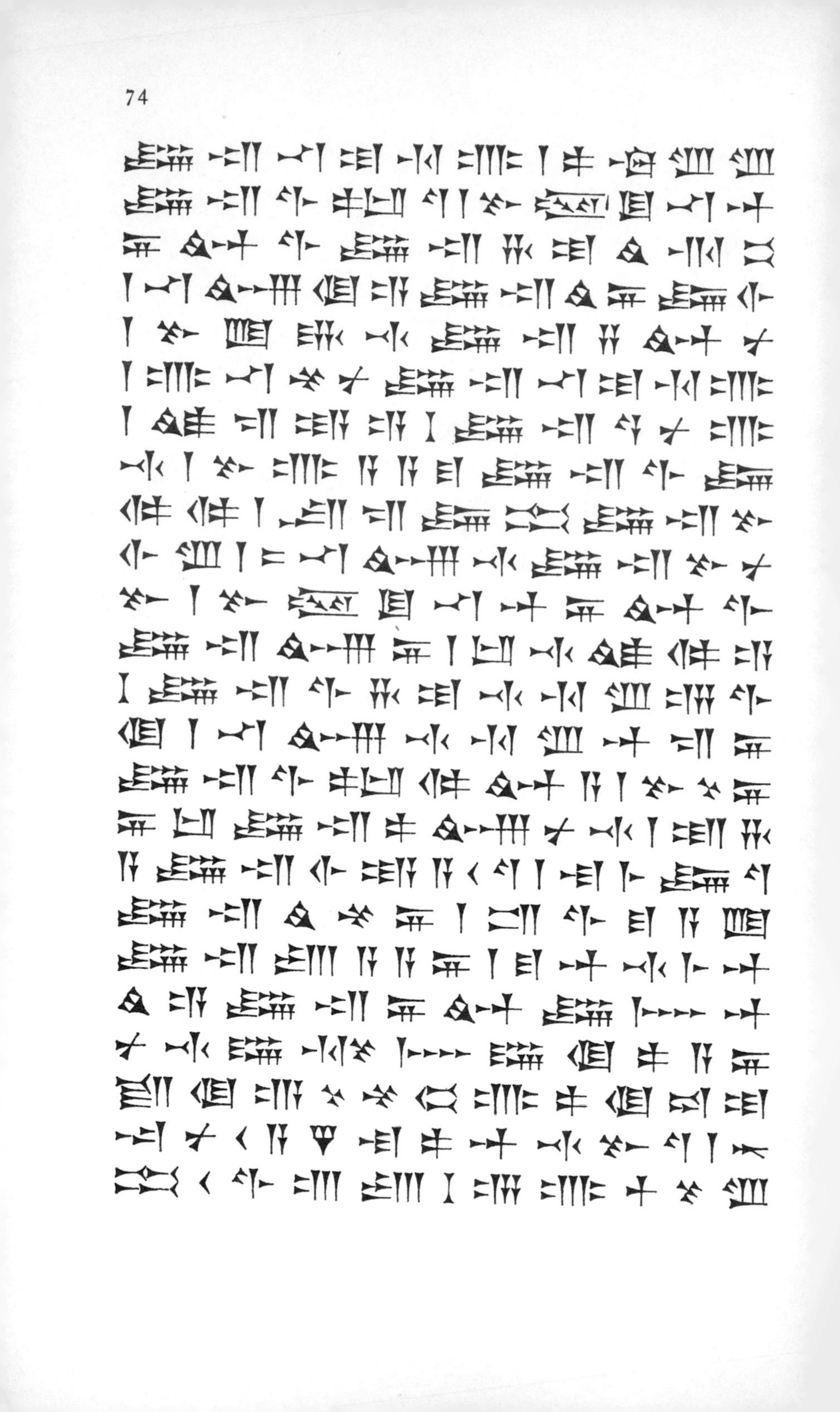

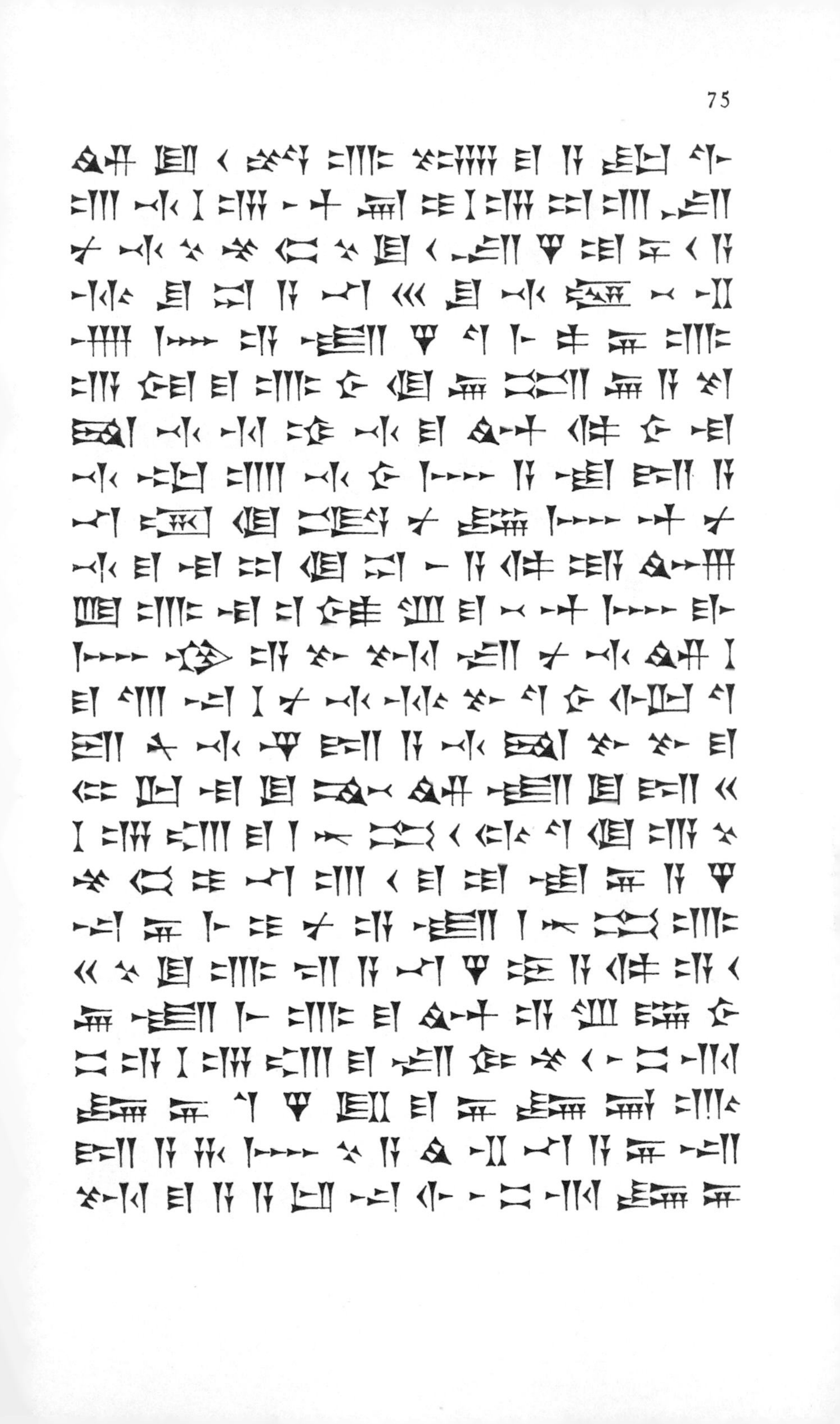

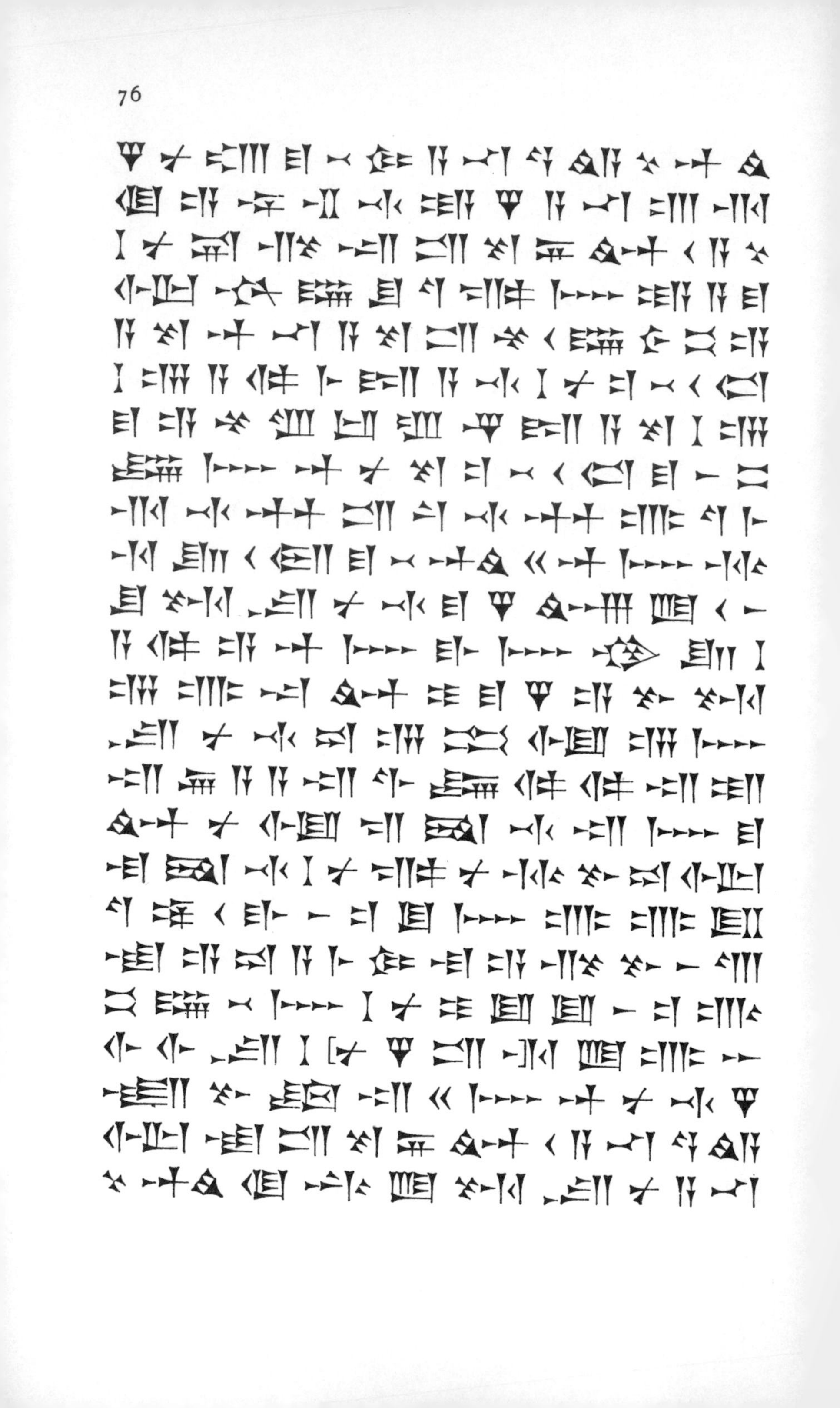

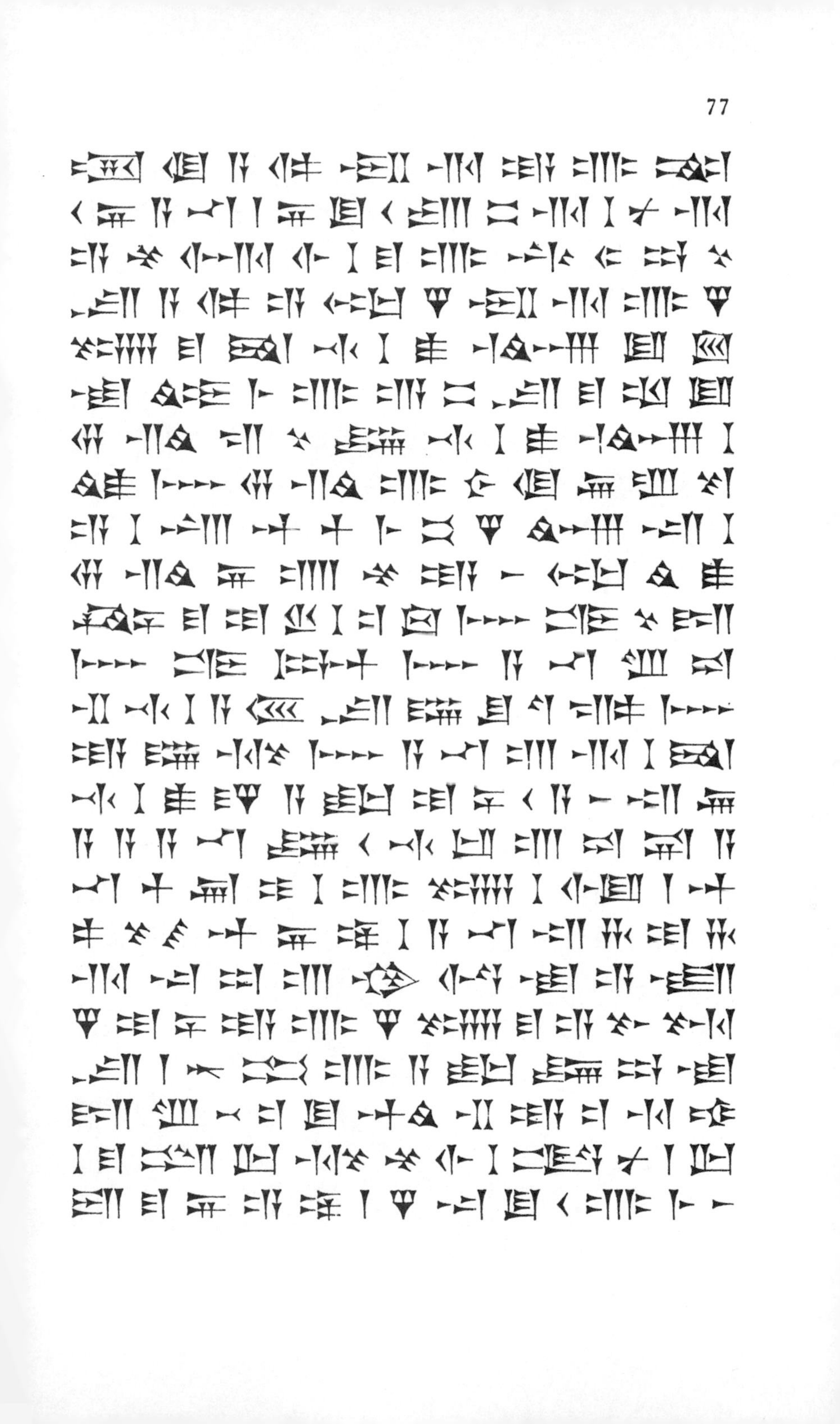

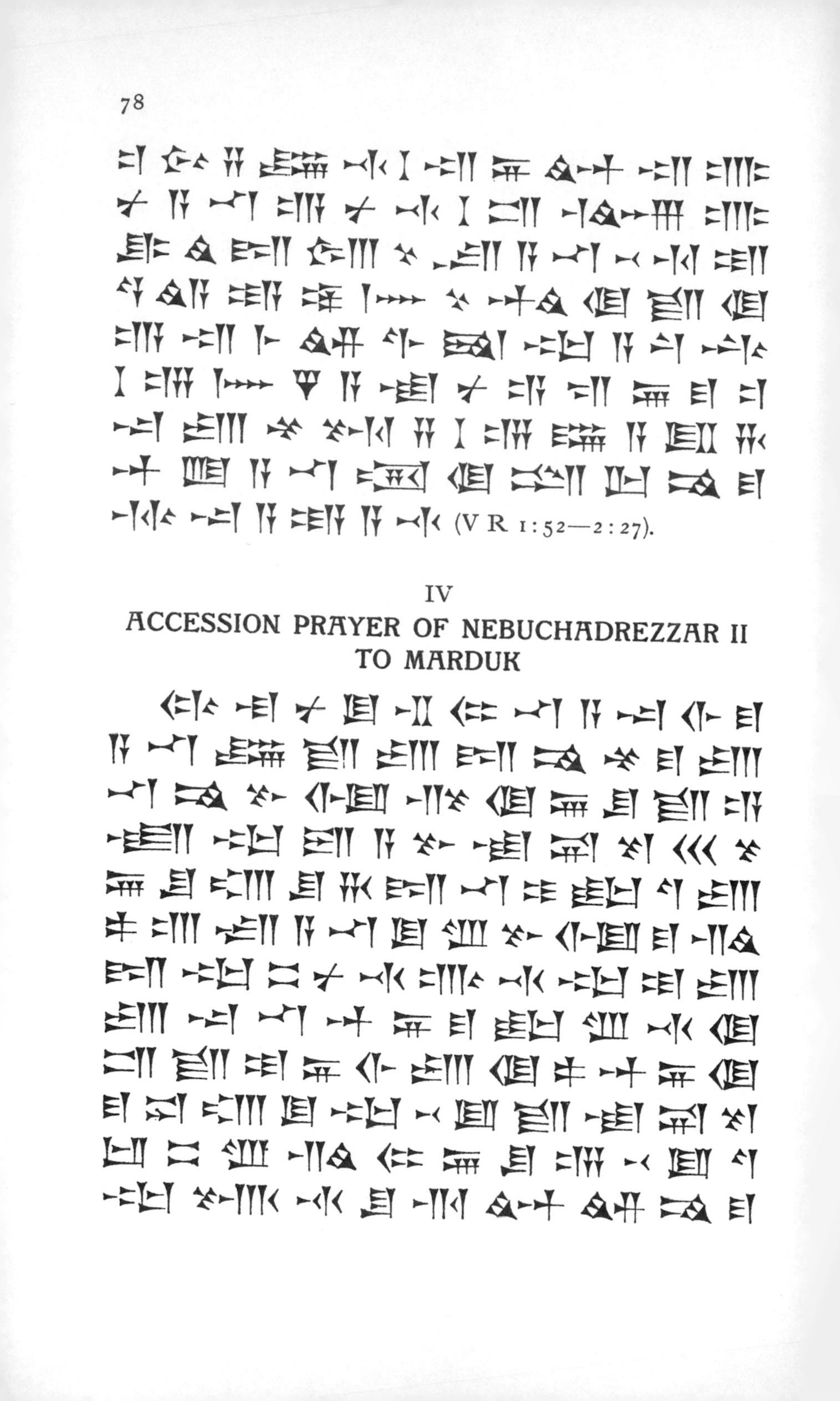

(V R 1:52—2:27).

IV

ACCESSION PRAYER OF NEBUCHADREZZAR II TO MARDUK

(I R 53, Col. I 55—II 1).

V

FROM IŠTAR'S DESCENT INTO HADES

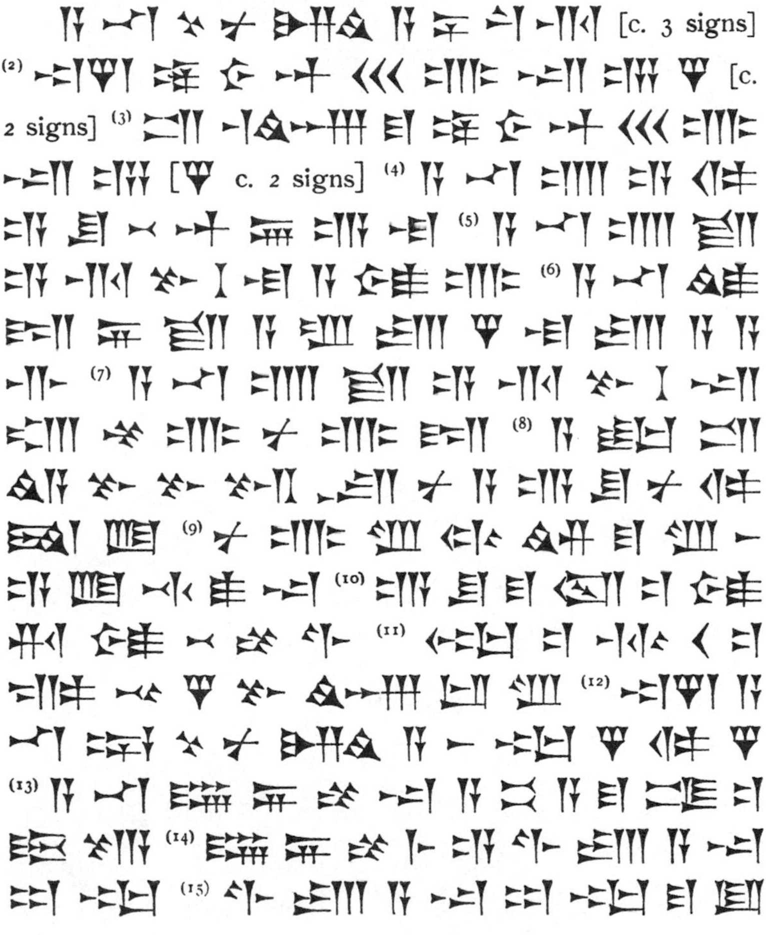
[c. 3 signs]
(2)
[c. 2 signs]
(3)
[c. 2 signs]
(4)
(5)
(6)
(7)
(8)
(9)
(10)
(11)
(12)
(13)
(14)
(15)

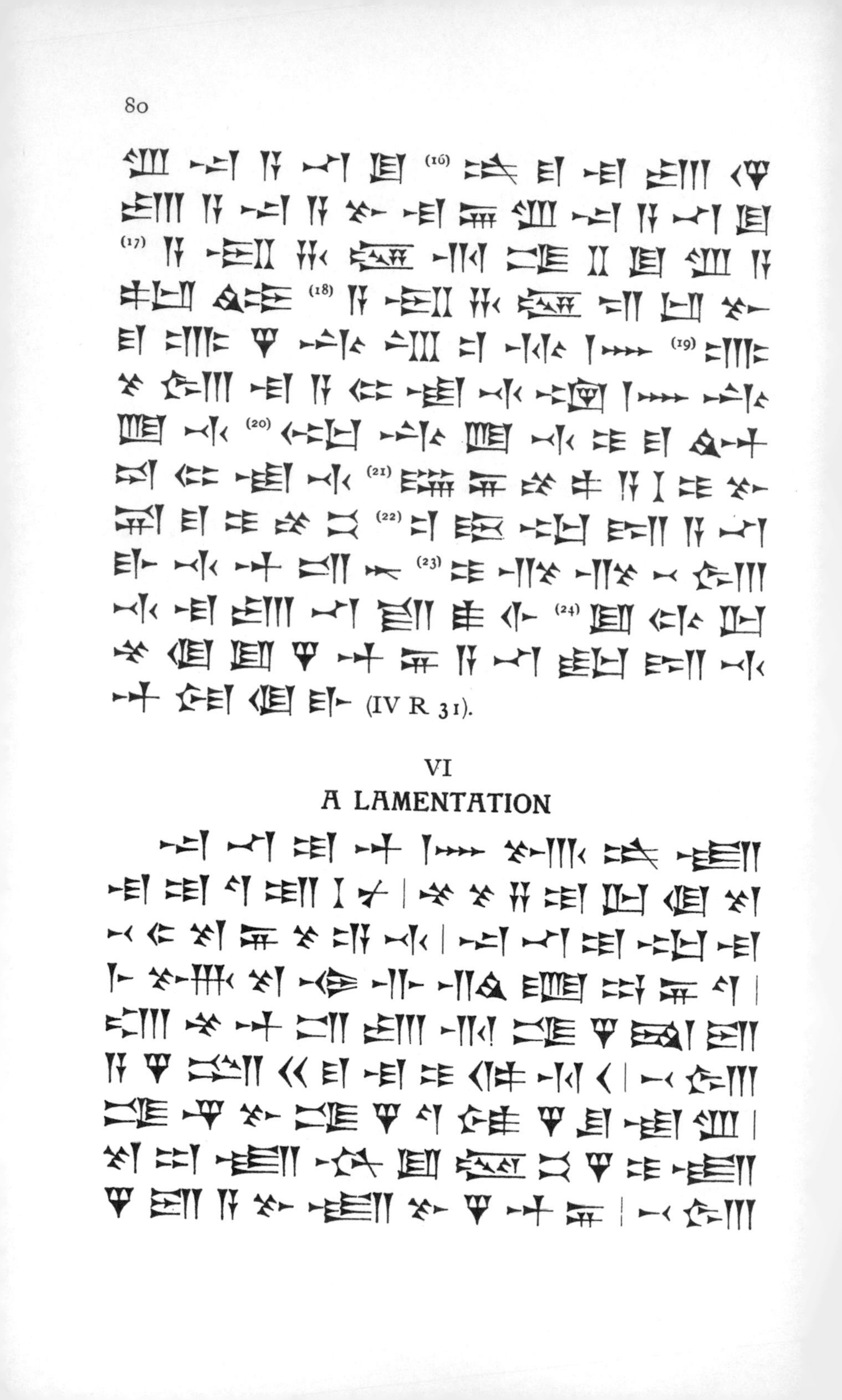

(IV R 31).

VI

A LAMENTATION

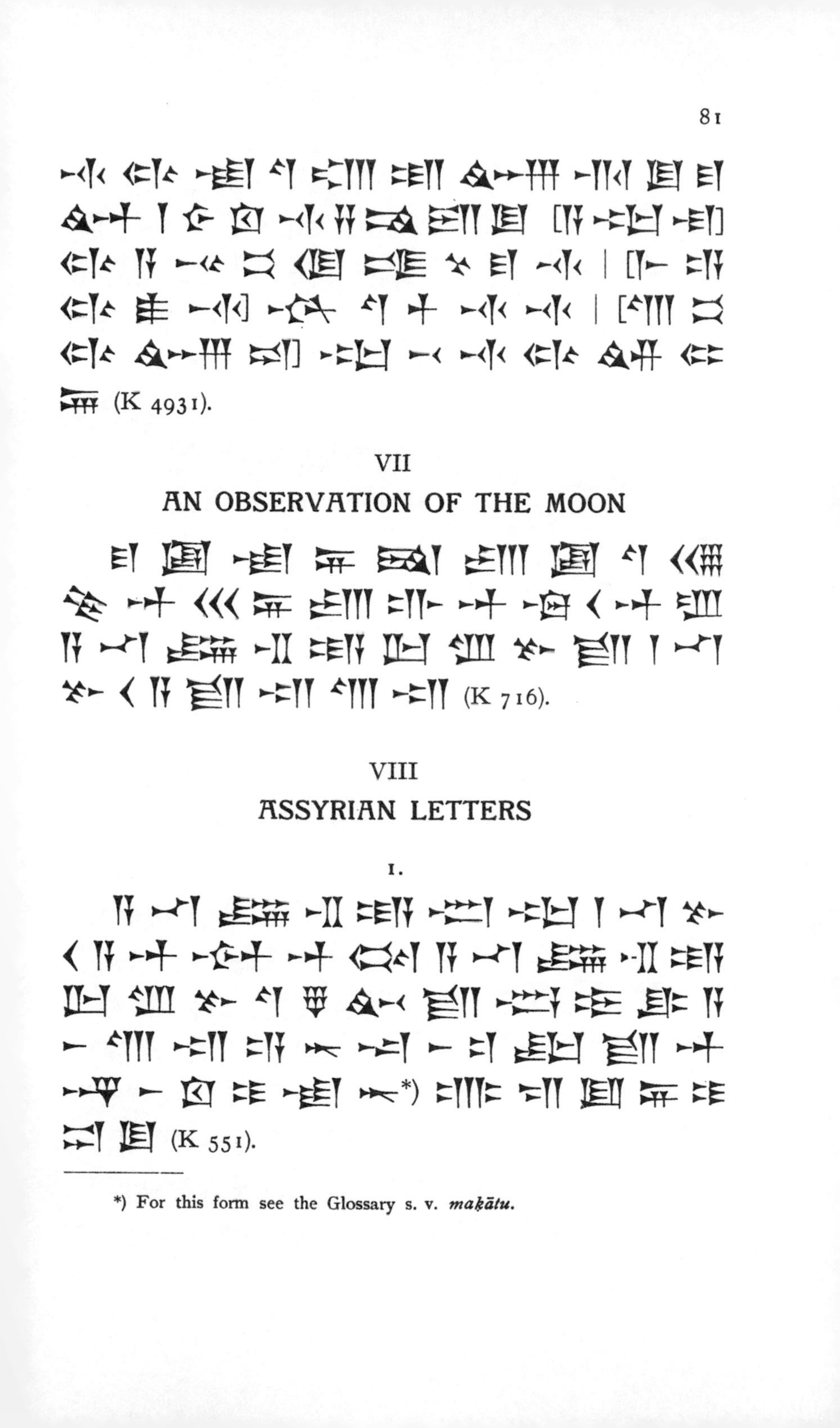

(K 4931).

VII

AN OBSERVATION OF THE MOON

(K 716).

VIII

ASSYRIAN LETTERS

I.

(K 551).

*) For this form see the Glossary s. v. *maḳātu*.

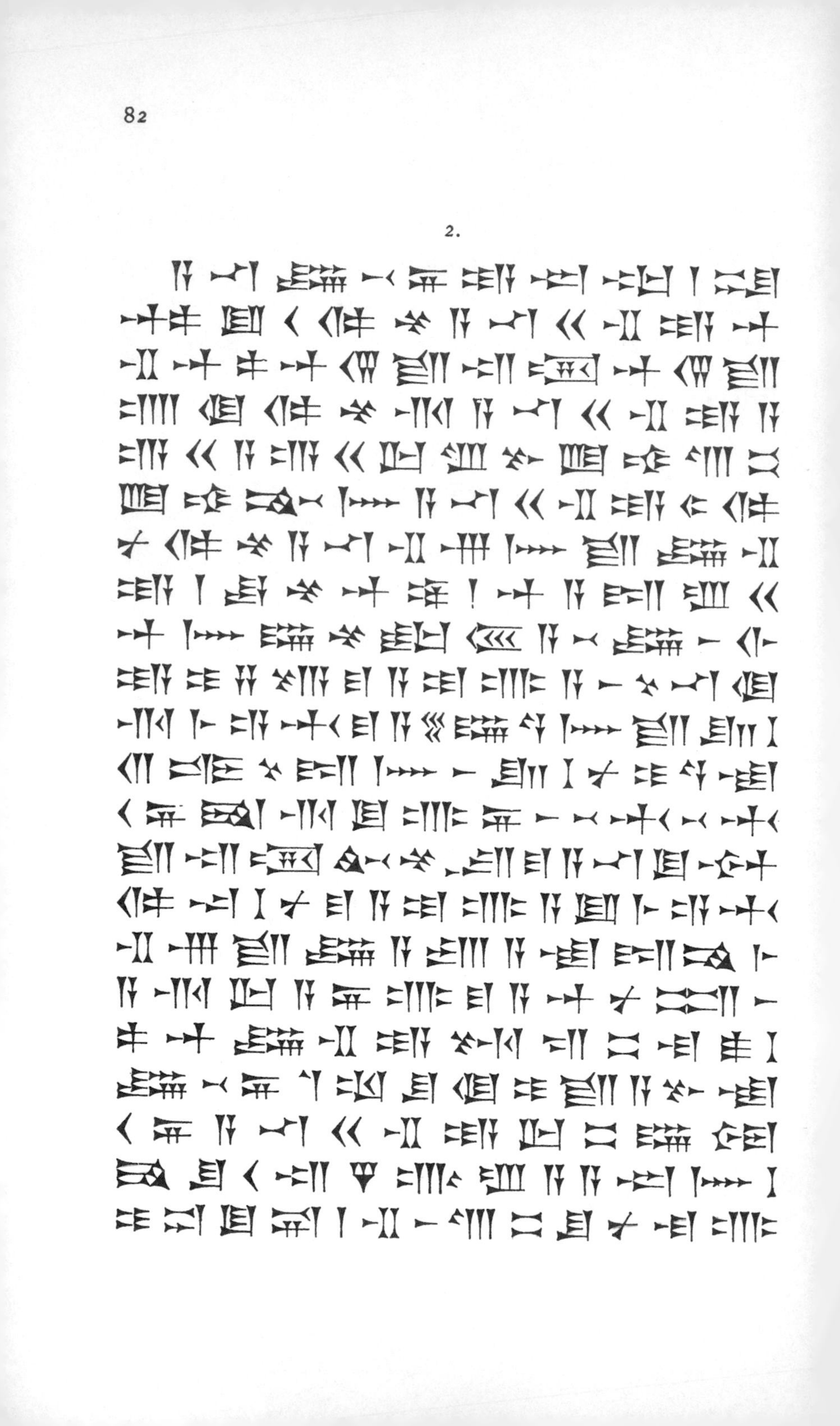

2.

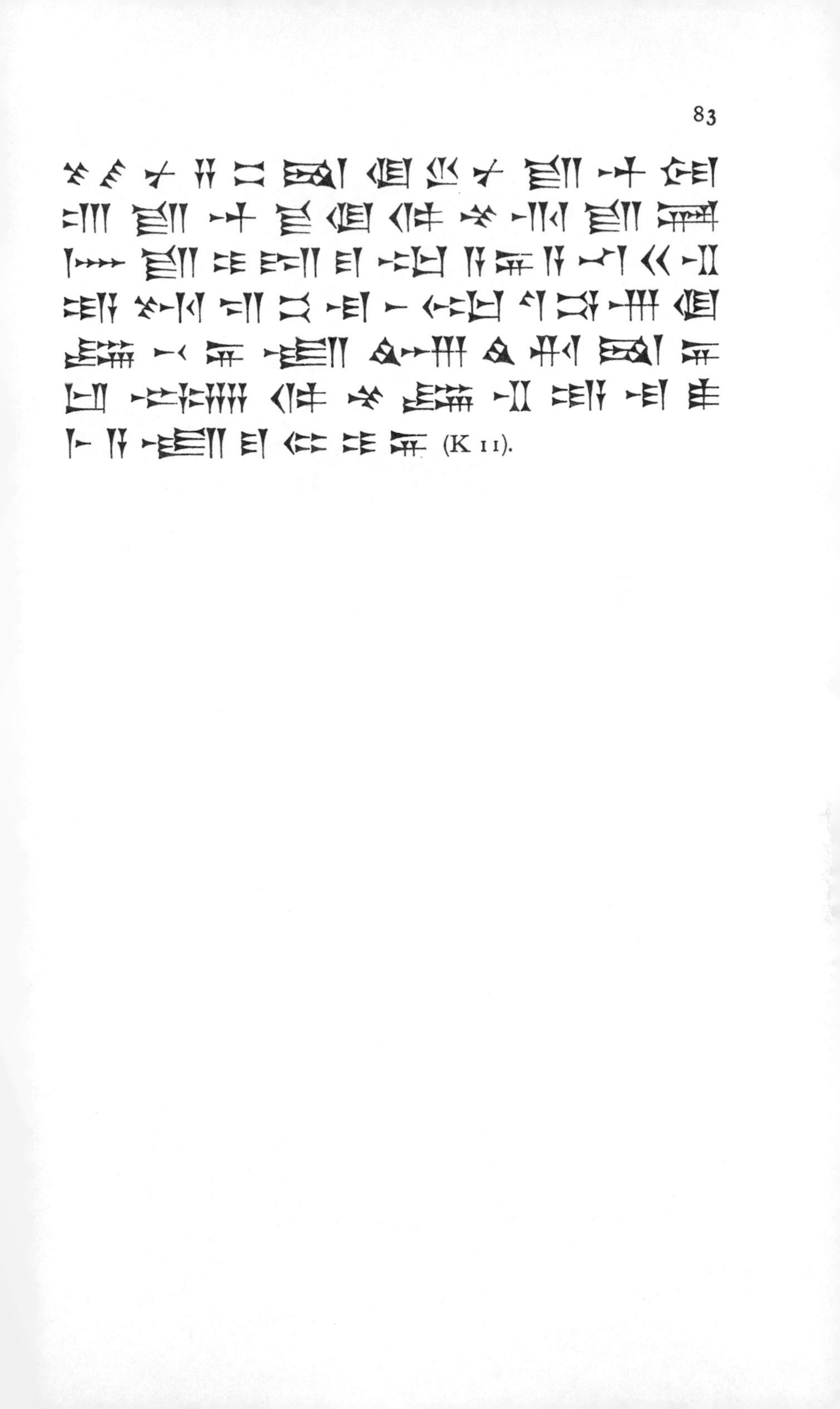

(K 11).

SIGN LIST*)

SIGN	SYLLABIC VALUES	IDEOGRAMS
1. [cuneiform]	*aš*, *rum*, *dil*, *ṭil*	*ina*, in; ([cuneiform]) [cuneiform] ([cuneiform]), Aššur, the land of Assyria: it is used also for the god Aššur, also for *nadānu*, to give, and for *aplu*, son, heir; ([cuneiform]) [cuneiform], ([cuneiform]) [cuneiform], *kussū*, throne.
2. [cuneiform]	*ḫal*	[cuneiform], sometimes used as sign for plural (e. g. [cuneiform] [cuneiform], *šumāti*, lines); [cuneiform] [cuneiform], *bārū*, seer; [cuneiform] [cuneiform] [cuneiform] [cuneiform], *Idiḳlat*, the Tigris.
3. [cuneiform]	*muk*, *muḳ*, *buk*, *puk*	
4. [cuneiform]	*ba*	[cuneiform], *ḳāšu*. to give.
5. [cuneiform]	*zu*	[cuneiform], *idū*, to know; *li'ū*, wise; [cuneiform] [cuneiform], *apsū*, abyss.

*) The numbers are those to be found in Delitzsch.

SIGN	SYLLABIC VALUES	IDEOGRAMS
6.  [cuneiform]	*su*, *kus*, *kuš*	*mašku*, skin; *erēbu*, to increase;  [cuneiform] [cuneiform], *ḫušāḫu*, *ḫušāḫḫu*, famine.
7.  [cuneiform]	*šin*, *šun*, *rug*, *ruk*, *ruḳ*	
8.  [cuneiform]	*bal*, *pal*	*palū*, year of reign; *nabalkutu*, to cross over; *enū*, to make void; *naḳū*, to pour out (a libation), to offer (a sacrifice); *šupēlu*, to conquer;  [cuneiform] [cuneiform] [cuneiform], the city *Aššur*.
9.  [cuneiform]	*ad*, *aṭ*, *at*, *gir*	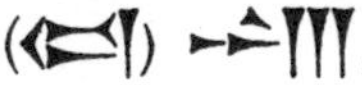 *paṭru*, dagger;  [cuneiform] [cuneiform], *aḳrabu*, scorpion; ([cuneiform]) [cuneiform], *birḳu*, lightning.
10.  [cuneiform]	*bul*, *pul*	(*pašāru*, to loosen.)
11. [cuneiform]	*tar*, *kut*, *ḳud*, *ḳut*, *ḳuṭ*, *šil*, *ḫaṣ*, *ḫaz*	*nakāsu*, to cut off; *parāsu*, to decide; *sūḳu*, street.
12.  [cuneiform]	*an*	    *ilu*, god; *šamū*, heaven; 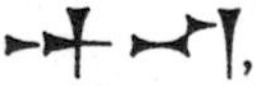 [cuneiform] [cuneiform], *anaku*, lead; [cuneiform] [cuneiform], *parzillu*, iron; [cuneiform] [cuneiform], *elū*, high; [cuneiform] [cuneiform], *atalū*, eclipse; [cuneiform] [cuneiform], *ṣēru*, field (orig. *Gir* or *Sumug*, the god of the field).

SIGN	SYLLABIC VALUES	IDEOGRAMS
13.		( ) , *Aššur*, the god; , *Aš-šur*, the city; ( ), *Aššur*, the country.
14.	*ka*	*pū*, mouth; *šinnu*, tooth; *amātu*, word; , *ḳibū*, to speak; *ḳibītu*, command; ( ), *suluppu*, date; , *kiṣru*, battalion.
14*a*.		*šiptu*, incantation; *nadū*, to pronounce a spell.
15.		*imtu*, breath; , *kaššapu*, sorcerer; , *kaššaptu*, sorceress.
17.		*taḫāzu*, battle (comp. No. 71).
18.		*lišānu*, tongue; ( ) , *Šumēr*.
19.	*nag*, *nak*, *naḳ*	*šatū*, to drink.
20.		*akālu*, to eat.
21.	*er* (*rí*, see p. 70)	*alu*, city.
23.	*ukkin*	*puḫru*, *unkennu*, totality, full strength.

SIGN	SYLLABIC VALUES	IDEOGRAMS
24.		( ) , *paššūru*, dish.
		, *šūtu*, the south wind, and comp. 185.
27.		*zikaru*, male; *ardu*, slave; , *Ura*, the plague-god; , the god *Ura-gal*.
28.		*arḫu*, month; e. g., , *Kislev*.
29.	*šaḫ*, *saḫ*, *šiḫ*	*šaḫū*, wild boar.
31.	*la*	
32.	(*pin*)	*uššu*, foundation; , *ikkaru*, gardener.
33.	*maḫ*	*ṣīru*, exalted; , *Ištar*.
34.	*tu*	*erēbu*, to enter; , *summatu*, dove.
35.	*li*	, *burāšu*, pine-tree.
36.	*bab*, *pap*, *kur*, *ḳur*	*nakāru*, to be hostile; *nakru*, hostile; *nakiru*, enemy; *napḫar*, total; in proper names it means *aḫu*, brother, and *naṣāru*, to protect.
47.	*kul*, *gul*, *ḳul*, *zir*	*zēru*, seed.

SIGN	SYLLABIC VALUES	IDEOGRAMS
37. [cuneiform]	*mu*	 *šumu*, name; *zakāru*, to name; *zikru*, name; *-ia*, first pers. pron.; in proper names, *nadānu*, to give;   [cuneiform] ([cuneiform] [cuneiform]), *šattu*, year; [cuneiform] [cuneiform], *musarū*, inscription.
38. [cuneiform]	*ḳa*	*ḳa*, a measure.
39. [cuneiform]	*kad*, *kaṭ*, *kat*	
40.  [cuneiform]	*gil*, *kil*	
41.  [cuneiform]	*kat*, *kad*	
43.  [cuneiform]	*ru*, *šub*, *šup*	*nadū*, to cast; *šumḳutu*, to conquest.
44. [cuneiform]	*be*, *bat*, *baṭ*, *bad*, *bit*, *mit*, *miṭ*, *mid*, *til*, *ziz*	 *mātu*, to die; *mītu*, *pagru*, corpse; *dāmu*, blood; [cuneiform] [cuneiform], *En-lil*, *Ea*.
45.  [cuneiform]	*na*	 ([cuneiform]) [cuneiform] [cuneiform] [cuneiform], *narū*, inscribed stone tablet.
46.  [cuneiform]	*šir*	   [cuneiform] [cuneiform] [cuneiform] [cuneiform], *Lagaš*; [cuneiform] [cuneiform] [cuneiform], *Šamaš*; [cuneiform] [cuneiform] [cuneiform] [cuneiform], *parūtu*, alabaster.
48.  [cuneiform], [cuneiform]	*ti*	  *laḳū*, *liḳū*, to take; [cuneiform] ([cuneiform]), *balāṭu*, to live.

SIGN	SYLLABIC VALUES	IDEOGRAMS
49. [cuneiform]	*bar*, (*par*), *maš*, *mas*	   *ašaridu*, chief;  ([cuneiform]) [cuneiform], *Ninib*; [cuneiform] [cuneiform] [cuneiform], *Nergal*; [cuneiform] [cuneiform] [cuneiform] [cuneiform] [cuneiform], *Idiḳlat*, *Diḳlat*, Tigris.
51. [cuneiform]	*nu*	*lā*, *ul*, not; *ṣalmu*, image;  [cuneiform] [cuneiform] [cuneiform] [cuneiform], *amēl urḳi*, *nukaribbu*, gardener; 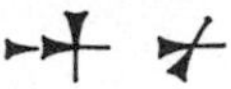  [cuneiform] [cuneiform] [cuneiform] [cuneiform], *Nu-dim-mud* (*Ea*).
52.  [cuneiform]		 *ṣibtu*, revenue; [cuneiform] [cuneiform], *šuttu*, dream.
53.  [cuneiform]	*kun*, *gun*	*zibbatu*, tail.
54.  [cuneiform], [cuneiform]	*ḫu*, *pag*, *pak*, *bag*, *bak*	*iṣṣūru*, bird.
55. 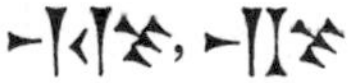 [cuneiform], [cuneiform]	*nan*, *nam*, *sim*	 *šīmtu*, fate; *paḫātu*, *piḫātu*, district;   [cuneiform] [cuneiform], *paḫātu*, governor; [cuneiform] [cuneiform], *si-nuntu*, swallow.
56.  [cuneiform], [cuneiform]	*ig*, *ik*, *iḳ*	*bašū*, to be;  ([cuneiform]) [cuneiform], *daltu*, door.
58.  [cuneiform], [cuneiform]	*mud*, *muṭ*, *mut*	
59.  [cuneiform]	*rad*, *raṭ*, *rat*	
60.  [cuneiform]	*zi*	*napištu*, life;  [cuneiform] [cuneiform], *imnu*, right; *kīnu*, true.

	SIGN	SYLLABIC VALUES	IDEOGRAMS
61.		*gi* (comp. 182)	*ḳanū*, reed; , *kānu*, to stand; *kīnu*, firm; , *dipāru*, torch.
62.	,	*ri*, *dal*, *ṭal*, *tal*	
63.	,	*nun*, *zil*, *ṣil*	*rubū*, noble; , *ab-kallu*, wise, master; , *Eridu*; , *Igigi*; comp. too , *tarbaṣu*, womb, hurdle.
65.		*kab*, *kap*	*šumēlu*, left.
66.		*ḫub*, *ḫup*	
67.		*kat*, *kad*, *gat*, *kum*, *ḳum*, *gum*	() , *kitū*, cloth.
68.		*tim*, *dim*	
69.		*mun*	*ṭābtu*, kindness.
70.		*ag*, *ak*, *aḳ*	*epēšu*, to make; *banū*, to build; and , *Nabū*.
71.			*taḫāzu*, battle (compare No. 17).
72.		*en*	*bēlu*, lord; *adi*, up to; (), *ma-ṣartu*, watch; , *kuṣṣu*, cold; ,

	SIGN	SYLLABIC VALUES	IDEOGRAMS
			[cuneiform], *Sin*; [cuneiform] [cuneiform], *Bēl*; [cuneiform] [cuneiform], *En-lil*; [cuneiform] [cuneiform] [cuneiform], *Nippur*; [cuneiform] [cuneiform] [cuneiform], *ḫazannu*, governor.
73.	[cuneiform]	*dar* (rare)	
74.	[cuneiform]	*šur*, *sur*	
75.	[cuneiform]	*suḫ*	
76.	[cuneiform]		[cuneiform] [cuneiform], [cuneiform] [cuneiform], *Ištar*.
78.	[cuneiform]	*sa*	
79.	[cuneiform]	*kar*, *kan*	*eḳlu*, field.
80.	[cuneiform]	*tik*, *tiḳ*, (*gu*)	*kišādu*, neck, bank; [cuneiform] [cuneiform], *gugallu*, director; [cuneiform] [cuneiform] [cuneiform] [cuneiform], *Kūtū*, Cuthah.
81.	[cuneiform]	*ṭur*, *dur*, *tur*	
82.	[cuneiform]		*biltu*, tribute, talent.
83.	[cuneiform]		*dišpu*, honey
84.	[cuneiform]	*gur*, *ḳur*	*tāru*, to turn; a measure.
85.	[cuneiform]	*si*	*ḳarnu*, horn; [cuneiform] [cuneiform], *ešēru*, to be straight; [cuneiform] [cuneiform] [cuneiform], *ištānu*, *iltānu*, the North Wind; ([cuneiform]) [cuneiform] [cuneiform] *šigaru*, lock, cage.

	SIGN	SYLLABIC VALUES	IDEOGRAMS
86.		*ṭar* (and comp. 241)	*burrumu*, brightly coloured; *birmu*, brightly coloured cloth.
87.		*šak*, *šaḳ*, *sag*, *riš*, *ris*	*rīšu*, head; , *ḳaḳḳadu*, head; , *ašaridu*, chief; , *šaḳū*, ruler; , *sikkūru*, bolt.
88.		*má*	, *elippu*, ship; , , *malaḫu*, sailor.
89.		*dir*, *ṭir*, *tir*, *mal*	
90.		*tab*, *tap*, *dap*, *ṭab*	
91.			*arba'u*, *irbitti*, four; , *Arba'-ilu*, Arbela.
92.		*tak*, *taḳ*, *tag*, *šum*, *šun*	*lapātu*, to turn, to overthrow.
93.		*ab*, *ap*, *eš*	
94.		*nab*, *nap*	
95.		*mul*	*kakkabu*, star.
96.		*ug*, *uk*, *uḳ*	
97.		*az*, *as*, *aṣ*	
98.			*erū*, copper.

SIGN	SYLLABIC VALUES	IDEOGRAMS
100.		*bābu*, gate; , *abullu*, city-gate; () (), *Bābilu*, Babylon.
101. ,		*Ninua*, *Ninā*, Nineveh.
102.	*um*	
103.	*dup*	*duppu*, tablet; *tabāku*, to pour out; , *dup-šimti*, tablet of destiny; () , *dup-šarru*, scribe.
104.	*ta*	*ištu*, *ultu*, from; , determinative after numbers and measures.
105.	*i*	*nā'idu*, *nādu*, exalted; () , *askuppu*, *askuppatu*, threshold.
107.	*kan*, *gan*	determinative after numbers (see 231); , *ḫegallu*, abundance.
	see	

SIGN	SYLLABIC VALUES	IDEOGRAMS
108.	*tur*	*ṣaḫru*, *ṣiḫru*, small; *māru*, son; , *aplu*, *māru*, son; , *mārtu*, *bintu*, daughter; () , *mārūtu*, sonship.
109.	*ad*, *aṭ*, *at*	*abu*, father.
110.	*ṣi*	
106.	*ia*	
111.	*in*	
112.	*rab*, *rap*	
114.		*šarru*, king; , *Marduk*.
115.	*šar*, *sar*, *šir*, *ḫir*	*šaṭāru*, to write; , *kirū*, plantation; , *ḳutaṣṣuru*, to collect, to rally.
116.		*dūru*, wall; (), *mītu*, dead.
117.	*se*, *šúm*	*nadānu*, to give; , *šūmu*, onion.
118.	*kas*, *raš*, *ras*	*ḫarrānu*, way; , *girru*, campaign; , *biru*, space of two hours.
120.	*gab*, *gap*, *ḳab*, *daḫ*, *duḫ*, *taḫ*, *tuḫ*	*irtu*, breast; () *gabrū*, *māḫiru*, rival.

	SIGN	SYLLABIC VALUES	IDEOGRAMS
121.			*ṣēru*, field; *ṣīr*, against.
122.		*daḫ*, *taḫ*	
123.		*am*	*rīmu*, wild ox; , *pīru*, elephant.
124.			*šīru*, flesh; oracle.
125.		*ne*, *ṭe*, *de*, *bil*, *pil*, *kum*, *ḳum*, *bi*	*išātu*, fire; *eššu*, new; , *Gibil*, fire-god.
126.		*bil*, *pil*	*eššu*, new.
127.		*zik*, *ziḳ*, *ṣip*	
128.			, *Uruk*, Erech.
129.		*ḳu*, *ḳum*	
130.		*gaz*, *gas*, *gaṣ*, *kas*	*dāku*, to slay.
132.		*ram*	*rāmu*, to love.
131.			*Ninua*, *Ninā*, Nineveh.
133.		*ur*	*sūnu*, loins; , *išid šamē*, the horizon.
134.			*išdu*, foundation.
135.		*il*	
136.		*du*, *gup*, *kup*, *ḳup*, *gub*, *kub*, *ḳub*, *kin*	*alāku*, to go; *nazāzu*, to stand; *kānu*, to stand; *kīnu*, true; , , *italluku*, to go.
138.		*tum*, *dum*, (*ib*)	

	SIGN	SYLLABIC VALUES	IDEOGRAMS
139.			*imēru*, ass, a measure; , *sisū*, horse; , , *parū*, mule; , , *gammalu*, camel.
140.			*arkū*, situated behind; future; *arki*, behind, after.
141.			, *karānu*, wine.
142.		*uš*, *nit*	*zikaru*, male; *šuššu*, sixty.
143.		*iš*, *mil*	*epiru*, *epru*, dust.
144.		*bi*, *kaš*, *gaš*, *kas*	*šikaru*, date-wine; , *kurunnu*, sesame-wine.
145.		*šim*, *rik*, *riḳ*, *rig*	*riḳḳu*, a sweet-smelling wood; () , *burāšu*, pine-tree.
146.		*kib*, *kip*, *ḳib*, *ḳip*	
147.		*tak*, *taḳ*, *dak*	*abnu*, stone.
148.		*kak*, *ḳaḳ*, *da*	*banū*, to build; *epēšu*, to make; *kalū*, all.
149.		*ni*, *zal*, *sal*, *ṣal*, *i*, *li*	*šamnu*, oil; , *pētū*, porter. Comp. too , *i-li*, my god.

	SIGN	SYLLABIC VALUES	IDEOGRAMS
150.	[cuneiform]	*ir*	
151.	[cuneiform]	*mal*	
152.	[cuneiform] ([cuneiform] in [cuneiform])		*rapāšu*, to be broad; *rapšu*, broad; *rupšu*, breadth; *ummu*, mother.
153.	[cuneiform], [cuneiform]		*kisallu*, platform; *šamnu*, oil.
154.	[cuneiform]		[cuneiform] [cuneiform], *gušūru*, beam.
155.	[cuneiform]		*milku*, counsel.
157.	[cuneiform]	*dak*, *daḳ*, *tak*, *par*	
158.	[cuneiform]	*pa*, *ḫat*, *ḫaṭ*	[cuneiform] [cuneiform], *ḫaṭṭu*, sceptre; [cuneiform] [cuneiform] [cuneiform], *iššakku*, ruler; [cuneiform] [cuneiform], *Nabū*, *elāt šamē*, the zenith.
159.	[cuneiform]		*parṣu*, command.
160.	[cuneiform]	*šab*, *šap*, *sap*	
161.	[cuneiform]		[cuneiform] [cuneiform], *Nusku*.
162.	[cuneiform]	*sib*, *sip*	([cuneiform]) [cuneiform], *rē'u*, shepherd.
163.	[cuneiform]	*iz*, *is*, *iṣ*, *giš*	*iṣu*, wood; *šutēšuru*, to direct (other wise [cuneiform] [cuneiform]); [cuneiform] [cuneiform], *kakku*, weapon; *tukultu*, help; see [cuneiform]; [cuneiform] [cuneiform], *uṣurtu*, boundary, end, sculpture; [cuneiform] [cuneiform], *ṣillu*,

SIGN	SYLLABIC VALUES	IDEOGRAMS
		shadow; , *sikkūru*, bolt; , *tuḳumtu*, *tuḳuntu*, *tuḳmatu*, opposition, battle; , *Gibil*, fire-god; *išātu*, fire.
164.		*alpu*, ox.
165.	*al*	
166.	*ub*, *up*, *ar*	*kibratu*, quarter of heaven.
167.	*mar*	(), *māt amurrī*, the Westernland; , *amurrū*, the west-wind; see .
168.	*e*	(), *Bābilu*, Babylon.
169.	*duk*, *lud*, *luṭ*, *lut*	*karpatu*, pot, vessel.
170.		*inbu*, fruit.
171.	*un*	*nišu*, people; , *šigrēti*, women of the palace (שֵׁגָל F. H.), syn. .
172.	*kid*, *kit*, *ḳid*, *ḳit*, *git*, *saḫ*, *siḫ*, *lil*	

	SIGN	SYLLABIC VALUES	IDEOGRAMS
173.		*rid*, *rit*, *šid*, *šit*, *lak*, *lak̦*, *mis*, *miṣ*, *mĭš*, *kil*	*minūtu*, number; ( ) , *šangū*, priest; , *kunukku*, seal; , *Marduk*.
174.		*u*, *šam*, *šan*	*rītu*, fodder; *ammatu*, an ell; *šammu*, plant.
175.		*ga*	*šizbu*, milk.
176.			*našū*, to raise.
177.		*laḫ*, *liḫ*, *luḫ*, *riḫ*	*sukkallu*, minister.
178.		*kal*, *rib*, *lab*, *lap*, *lib*, *lip*, *dan*, *ṭan*, *tan*	*dannu*, mighty; *danniš*, exceedingly; , *lamassu*, sacred colossal bull; , *ušū*, a precious wood; ( ) , *idlu*, man, lord.
179.			, *šēdu*, sacred colossal bull; , *karāšu*, camp.
180.		*bit*, *biṭ*, *pit*; *e* (rare)	*bītu*, house; , *šangū*, priest; , *ekallu*, palace; , *ekurru*, temple; , *igaru*, wall.
181.		*nir*	

SIGN	SYLLABIC VALUES	IDEOGRAMS
182.	*gi* (rare), comp. 61	(), *tāru*, to turn.
183.	*ra*	
185.		*amēlu*, man; , *amēlu*, man.
186.	*šiš*, *šis*, *sis*, *siš*	*aḫu*, brother; *naṣāru*, to protect; , *Nannaru*, *Sin*; , *Uri*, the city Ur.
187. ()	*zak*, *zaḳ*	*imnu*, right; *pāṭu*, boundary; *pūtu*, front, face.
	see	
	see	
188.	*ḳar*, *gar*	
189.	*id*, *iṭ*, *it*	*idu*, hand; , *našru*, eagle; , *li'ū*, strong.
190.	*lil*	
191.		*ḳablu*, midst, battle.
192.	*da*, *ṭa*	, *dārū*, everlasting; , *dannu*, mighty.
193.	*aš*	

SIGN	SYLLABIC VALUES	IDEOGRAMS
194.	*ma*	, *mātu*, land; , *adanniš*, exceedingly; , *manū*, maneh.
195.	*gal*, *ḳal*	*rabū*, great; , *ušumgallu*, monster-viper; , *rab-ḳiṣir*, captain; , an officer (chief of the bakers); , *rab-šaḳē*, an officer (cup-bearer?); , *rab-ešrēti*, chief over ten, decurio; , *rab-āsē*, chief-astrologer.
196.	*bar*	*parakku*, shrine.
197.	*biš*, *piš*, *kir*, *gir*	
198.	*mir*	*agū*, crown; *izzu*, angry, terrible.
199.		() , *nāgiru*, commander.
200.	*bur*, *pur*	
		see (136)

	SIGN	SYLLABIC VALUES	IDEOGRAMS
201.			*bēltu*, lady.
202.			*arku*, yellow, green.
203.		*dub*, *tup*	
204.		*šá*	
205.		*šu*, *kat*, *ḳat*	*ḳātu*, hand; , *ubānu*, finger;  , Babylon; , *napḫaru*, total;  , *šutšaḳē*, officer.
207.		*lul*, *lib*, *lip*, *lup*, *pah*, *nar*	, *zammeru*, male musician; , *zammertu*, *nārtu*, female musician; , *šēlibu*, fox.
206.		*sa* (rare)	*damāḳu*, to be favourable; , *gišimmaru*, date-palm.
208.			*ṣalmu*, image.
209.			, Akkad (sometimes *Urarṭu*, Armenia).
210.		*gam*, *ḳam*, *gur*	
		see 201 and 202	

	SIGN	SYLLABIC VALUES	IDEOGRAMS
211.		*kur*, *mat*, *mad*, *šad*, *šaṭ*, *šat*, *lat*, *nat*, *nad*, *kin*	*mātu*, land, country; *šadū*, mountain; *kašādu*, to conquer; *napāḫu*, to shine forth; *šadū*, the east-wind.
212.		*še*	*šeu*, grain; , *magāru*, to be obedient to; , *šamaššammu*, sesame-seed.
213.		*bu*, *pu*, *sir*, (*šir*), *git*, *ḳit*	, *arku*, long.
214.		*uz*, *us*, *uṣ*	
215.		*šud*, *šut*, *sir*	*rūḳu*, distant.
216.		*muš*, *ṣir*	*ṣiru*, serpent;  , *mušruššū*, red dragon (comp. Revel. 12, 3).
217.		*tir*	*kištu*, wood.
218.		*te*	*temenu*, foundation-stone; *ṭaḫū*. *ṭeḫū*, to be near; , *gallū*, devil; 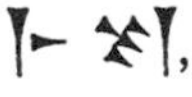, see 293.
219.		*kar*	*kāru*, wall; *eṭēru*, to protect.
220.		*liš*, *lis*	

SIGN	SYLLABIC VALUES	IDEOGRAMS
221. 𒑱		a sign used for marking the division of words (orig. for equation).
222. 𒌓	*ud*, *uṭ*, *ut*, *u*, *tu*, *tam*, *bir*, *par*, *pir*, *laḫ*, *liḫ*, *ḫiš*, *ḫis*	*ūmu*, day; *ūmu*, dragon; *šamšu*, sun; *ṣītu*, exit; *piṣū*, white; 𒀭 𒌓, *Šamaš*; 𒌓 𒂊, *aṣū*, to go forth; 𒀭 𒌓 𒌓 𒂊, *ṣīt šamši*, sun-rise; 𒀭 𒌓 𒋗 𒀀, *erēb šamši*, sun-set; 𒌓 𒅗 𒁇, *siparru*, bronze; 𒌓 𒀕 𒆠, *Larsam*; 𒌓 𒄒 𒉣 𒆠, *Sippar*; 𒀀 𒇉 𒌓 𒄒 𒉣 (𒆠), *Purātu*, Euphrates; 𒌓 𒉌, *urru*, light.
223. 𒉿	*pi*, *tal* (rare), babyl. also *ya*, *yi*, *wa*, *wi* (later *ma*, *mi*)	*uznu*, ear.
224. 𒊮	*lib*	*libbu*, heart; 𒊮 𒁄 𒁄, *līplīpi*, descendant; (𒌷) 𒊮 𒌷, the city Aššur.
225. 𒌔	*uḫ*	*rū'tu*, *rūtu*, spittle.

SIGN	SYLLABIC VALUES	IDEOGRAMS
226.	*ṣab*, *ṣap*, *zab*, *bir*, *pir*, *laḫ*, *liḫ*	*ṣābu*, warrior; *ummānu*, host; *niraru*, helper.
		pir'u, offspring.
227.	*zib*, *zip*, *ṣip*	
228.	*ḫi*, *ṭi*, *šar*	*kiššatu*, host, the world; *ṭābu*, good; the god Aššur; Assyria; *Eridu*.
229.	*'a*, *'i*, *'u*, *a'*, *i'*, *u'*	
230.	*aḫ*, *iḫ*, *uḫ*	
231.	*kam*, *ḫam*	determinative after numbers (= , comp. 107).
232.	*im*	*šāru*, wind; *šūtu*, south-wind; *ištānu*, *iltānu*, north-wind; *amurrū*, west-wind; *šadū*, east-wind; *imḫullu*, evil

SIGN	SYLLABIC VALUES	IDEOGRAMS
		wind; , the god *Adad* (babyl. *Rammān*); , *irpitu*, *urpatu*, cloude; , *nā'idu*, *nādu*, exalted.
233. 	*bir*, *pir*	*sapāḫu*, to bring to naught.
234. 	*ḫar*, *ḫir*, *ḫur*, *mur*, *kin*	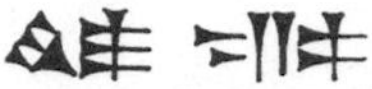, *šadū*, mountain-range.
235. 	*ḫuš*, *ruš*	*ruššū*, red; *izzu*, angry (and comp. 216).
237. 	*ṣun*	*ma'ādu*, *mādu*, many; sign of plural.
238. 	*u*	, the god *Adad* or *Rammān*.
239. 	*muḫ*	*eli*, over, upon.
240. 		, *Nergal*.
241. 	(comp. 86)	, *ištar*, goddess; *Ištar*.
242. 	*lid*, *liṭ*, *lit*, *rim*	
243. 	*kir*	
244. 	*kiš*, *kis*, *ḳiš*	*kiššatu*, host, the world.
245. 	*mi*	*mūšu*, night; *ṣalmu*, dark.
246. 	*gul*, *kul*, *ḳul*, *sun*	

	SIGN	SYLLABIC VALUES	IDEOGRAMS
247.			, *iršu*, couch.
248.		*nim*, *num*; *tum* (rare)	, *Elam*.
249.		*tum*	
250.		*lam*, *lim* (?)	
252.		*zur*, *ṣur*	, *Marduk*.
253.			, *nikū*, offering.
254.		*ban*, *pan*	, *ḳaštu*, bow.
255.		*kim*, *gim*, *dim*	*kīma*, like, as.
256.		*ul*	
257.			*šēpu*, foot; , *šakkanakku*, *šakkanaku*, governor; , bones; , *ṣēru*, field; , *Nergal*.
258.			*kabtu*, heavy.
259.		*gig*, *kik*	*marṣu*, sick.
260.		*ši*, *lim*	*īnu*, eye; *pānu*, face; *maḫru*, front; *amāru*, to see; , *amāru*, to see; , *abiktu*, defeat; , *Ninib*, *Nergal*.

	SIGN	SYLLABIC VALUES	IDEOGRAMS
262.		*ar*	
263.			*tukultu*, help; *ittu*, sign.
264.			*damāḳu*, to be favourable; *damḳu*, favourable; *dumḳu*, *dunḳu*, favour; ( ) , *damiḳtu*, mercy, favour.
265.		*u*	*u*, and; , *ašūḫu*, a tree.
266.		*ḫul*	*limnu*, evil; ( ) , *limuttu*, evil.
267.	,	*di*, *ṭi*	*šalāmu*, to be complete; *šulmu*, prosperity; , *daianu*, judge; , *sattukku*, regular offering; , *šanānu*, to equal; , *Šulmānu*, the god *Šulmān*.
268.	,	*tul*, *til*	*tilu*, mound.
269.		*ki*	*irṣitu*, earth; *ašru*, place; *itti*, with; , *dannatu*, distress; , *šaplu*, under part, low;

	SIGN	SYLLABIC VALUES	IDEOGRAMS
			(or [cuneiform]) [cuneiform], *Šumēr*; [cuneiform] [cuneiform], *šubtu*, dwelling; [cuneiform] [cuneiform], *šuḳultu*, weight (?).
270. 	[cuneiform]		sign of repetition, *ditto*.
271.	[cuneiform]	*din, tin*	*balāṭu*, to live;   [cuneiform] [cuneiform] [cuneiform], *Bābilu*, Babylon.
272.	[cuneiform]	*šik, šiḳ, sik, zik, pik, piḳ*	var. of [cuneiform].
273. 	[cuneiform]	*dun, šul, sul*	
274.	[cuneiform]		*ellu*, bright; [cuneiform] [cuneiform], *ḫurāṣu*, gold; [cuneiform] [cuneiform], *kaspu, ṣarpu*, silver.
275. 	[cuneiform]	*pad, paṭ, pat, šuk, šuḳ*	*kurummatu*, food;   [cuneiform] [cuneiform], *nindabū*, free-will offering.
276. 	[cuneiform]		*imnu*, right; [cuneiform] [cuneiform], *ištar*, goddess, Ištar (number fifteen).
277.	[cuneiform]	*man, niš*	*šarru*, king; *Šamaš* (number twenty).
278*a* 	[cuneiform]	*eš, sin*	  ([cuneiform]) [cuneiform], *Sin* (number thirty);  [cuneiform], *purussū*, decision.
278*b*	[cuneiform]		 ([cuneiform]) [cuneiform], *Enlil* (number fifty).

	SIGN	SYLLABIC VALUES	IDEOGRAMS
279.		*diš, tiš, tis, ṭis, ana*	*ana*, to; *ištēn*, one; *enuma*, when; determinative before proper names.
280.		*lal, la*	*šaḳālu*, to weigh; *ṣimittu*, yoke; *kamū*, to bind, to catch. Comp. no. 269.
282.		*kil, ḳil, gil, rim, rin, ḫab, ḫap, kir*	
283.			, *nāru*, river.
284.			, *narkabtu*, chariot.
285.			, *iddū*, bitumen; , *kupru*, bitumen.
286.		*zar, ṣar*	
287.		*u*	, *ṣēnu*, sheep.
288.		*pu, ṭul*	*būru*, well, spring.
289.		*bul, pul*	
290.		*zuk, zuḳ, suk*	
291.			*puḫḫuru*, to collect; , *napḫaru*, whole, total.
292.			*annanna*, "so and so".

	SIGN	SYLLABIC VALUES	IDEOGRAMS
293.		*me, šib, šip, sip*	 is sometimes used for ; , *simtu*, ornament (*simat* worthy of).
294.		*meš, miš*	sign of the plural.
295.		*ib, ip*	
296.		*ku, dur, tuk* (rare), *tuš*	*tukultu*, help; *ṣubātu*, garment; *ašābu*, to dwell; , *ulinnu*, a garment; , *kakku*, weapon; *urkarinnu*, box-tree; , *miṭṭu*, club(?).
297.		*lu, dib, ṭib, tib*	*ṣabātu*, to take; *ṣēnu*, sheep; , *immeru*, lamb, sheep.
299.		*ḳi, ḳin, kin*	*šipru*, letter; *mu'uru*, to send, to rule.
300.		*šik*	*šipātu*, wool; *šārtu*, hair.
301.			, *erinu*, cedar.
302.		*šu*	*kiššatu*, host, the world; , *Marduk*.
303.			*šiptu*, incantation.
		*di, ṭi*	*šalāmu*, to be complete, etc.; see , no. 267
			see .

SIGN	SYLLABIC VALUES	IDEOGRAMS
304.		*šarāpu*, to burn.
305.		, *nīru*, yoke.
306.		*ḫidūtu*, joy.
307.	*šal, sal, rag, rak, min, mim*	*sinniš*, *sinništu*, female, wife; , *nukurtu*, hostility; , see ; , *limuttu*, evil; , *mimma*, anything. Comp. too 171.
308.	*ṣu, rik*	
309.	*nin*	*bēltu*, lady; , *Allatu*, a goddess; , *Nin-lil* (wife of *En-lil*).
310.	*dam, ṭam*	*aššatu*, wife.
311.	*gu*	, *kussū*, throne; , *guzalū*, shepherd (?), messenger; , *Bau.*
313.		*naggaru*, *nangaru*, a workman (smith ?).
312.	*amat* (only in *Ti-amat*)	*amtu*, maid.

	SIGN	SYLLABIC VALUES	IDEOGRAMS
314.		*nik*, *niḳ*	
315.		*el*	
316.		*lum*, *ḫum*; *kus*(?)	
317.			*libittu*, brick; *lipittu*, enclosure.
		see 272	
318.			number *two*.
319.		*tuk*, *tuḳ*	*išū*, to have; used in proper names for *šubšū*, to create.
320.		*ur*, *lik*, *liḳ*, *taš*, *tas*, *daš*, *das*, *tiš*, *tiz*, *tiṣ*	, *nēšu*, lion; , *barbaru*, wolf; , *ḳardu*, *ḳarradu*, strong; , *kalbu*, dog; , *šidimmu*(?), raging hound (name of a star).
322.			*šumēlu*, left (number hundred fifty).
323.		*a*	*mū*, water; *aplu*, son; *māru*, son; , *zanānu*, to rain; , , determinatives after numbers and measures;

	SIGN	SYLLABIC VALUES	IDEOGRAMS
			, *tiāmatu*, *tāmtu*, *tāmdu*, sea; , *mīlu*, flood; , *ugāru*, land; , *eḳlu*, field; , *bakū*, to weep; *bikītu*, weeping; , *nāru*, river; , *Purātu*, Euphrates; , see ; , see ; () , *āsū*, seer; , *nāḳ-mē*, irrigator; , *mār-šipri*, messenger.
324.		*ai*	, *Ai*, a goddess.
325.		*za*, *ṣa*	, *uknū*, lapis lazuli; , *ṣipru*, a kind of lapis lazuli.
326.		*ḫa*	*nūnu*, fish; , *ḫalāḳu*, to be destroyed.
327.		*gug*	
		šik, *šiḳ*, *sik*, *zik*, *pik*, *piḳ*	see no. 272 (var.).

SIGN	SYLLABIC VALUES	IDEOGRAMS
 [cuneiform]		*ḫammamu*, quarter of heaven.
328.  [cuneiform]	*ṭu*	*šiḳlu*, shekel.
329.  [cuneiform]		*šarru*, king.
330. [cuneiform]	*ša*, *gar*	    *šakānu*, to set; *šiknu*, image; *akālu*, food;  [cuneiform] [cuneiform], *makkūru*, property; [cuneiform] [cuneiform], *kudurru*, boundary, service;  [cuneiform] [cuneiform], *bušū*, property; [cuneiform] [cuneiform], *mešrū*, wealth; ([cuneiform]) [cuneiform], *šaknu*, governor; [cuneiform] [cuneiform] [cuneiform], *ḫaṭṭu*, sceptre.
332. [cuneiform]	*ia* (number five)	 [cuneiform] [cuneiform] [cuneiform], *Igigi*, the spirits of heaven.
333. [cuneiform]	*aš*	number six.

GLOSSARY

A

Abālu, to bring, III_2 *ussibil*
abātu, to do thoroughly, IV, to flee
abiktu, defeat
abītu, will, command
abu, father
adanniš, greatly
adi, together with, as far as
adī, compact
admānu, house
agāgu, to be enraged
agāru, to hire
aḫamiš, each other
aḫāzu, to hold
aḫinna = ***aḫi***, side, and *anna*, this
aḫu, side
aḫū, hostile
akālu, to eat, food
alaktu, way
alāku, to go
alālu, to hang up
alī-ma, where?
allaku, courier
allu, a chain
amāru, to see
amātu, affair, word
amēlu, man
ana, to
annušim, now
aplu, son
aplūtu, sonship
apparu, swamp
arādu, to go down, set out
arba'u, four
ardu, slave
arḫu, month
arkānu, afterwards
ašābu, to dwell
ašar, where
asāru, to besiege (comp. *esēru*)
ašru, place
aššurītu, the Assyrian
aṣū, go out, to go up
atāru, to increase (and comp. *šūturu*)
attūni, as for us

E

ebēru, to cross, III_2 to extend over
edu, alone, one
ēlēnū, upper
eli, more than
elū, to be high, to depart, II_1 to raise, III_1 to bring up
emēdu, II_1 to erect
emūku, force, army (comp. *imūku*)
epēšu, to do, make (comp. *ipištu*)
epiru, dust, earth (comp. *ipru*)
epištu, plu. *ipšatu*, deed
erēbu, to enter (comp. *irub*)
esēru, to besiege (comp. *asāru*)

ešēru, to guide, III_2 direct, make straight
eššūtu, newness
etēḳu, to march (and comp. *metiḳu*)
ezēbu, to leave, to deliver, III_1 to save
ezēzu, to make strong

I

idu, side
idū, to know
iḫzu, hilt
ikīmu, seize
ili, against
ilippu, ship
ilu, god
ilūtu, divinity
imūḳu, power, force (comp. *emēḳu*)
ina, *in*, with
īnu, eye
ipištu, deed (comp. *epištu*)
ipru, dust (comp. *epiru*)
irṣitu, earth
irubma, *irumma*, comp. *erēbu*
išaru, straight
išāru, III_2 see *ešēru*
išātu, fire
išḳatu, fetter
iṣṣūru, bird
ištaritum, a goddess
išteni'iu, I_3 to devise (of שׁעה)
iṣu, wood
ittu, with
iṭū, darkness

U

uba'i, of בעה, to seek (see *ba'ū*)
ullānu, without
ultu, out of
umā, so
ummānu, people, plu. troops
ummu, mother
ūmu, day
ūmu, *ina umēšuma*, at that time
umussu, daily
urḫu, road
urḳītu, green herb
urruḫiš, quickly
ušmānu, camp
uznu, ear

B

ba'ū, II_1 to seek
bābu, gate
bakū, to weep
balāṭu, live, spare
balkātu, III_1 to tear down
balṭu, alive
banat, mother
banū, to found, to build, to make
bašū, to be, to happen, III_1 place
battibatti, in the neighbourhood
bēlu, to take possession of, to rule; lord
bēltu, lady
biltu, present
bilu, to take possession of, see *bēlu*
birinni, between us
birītu, bond
birmi, variegated (stuffs)
bitḫallu, saddle-horse
bītu, house
bubūtu, bread

G

gamru, complete
gappu, feather
gašīšu, stake
gibšu, multitude
gimru, all
girru, expedition

D

dabābu, to device
dababtu, device
dagālu, to see
dagālu pan, to be subject to
dakū, to muster
dāku, to kill

daltu, door
damāḳu, to be favourable
damiḳtu, favour
damḳaru, name of a profession
damḳu, favourable
danānu, might
dannu, mighty, strong
dannūtu, fortress
dārū, *ana dārātim*, continuously, for ever
dikū, assemble
dimtu, tears
dīnu, judgement
dumḳu, mercy
dunḳu, favour
dūru, wall

Z

za'ānu, to adorn (see *ṣānu*)
zaḳāpu, to set up (and II_1)
zakāru, to address, to speak
zanānu, to send rain
zikaru, man
zikru, name
zummū, deprived

Ḫ

ḫabātu, plunder
ḫadū, to rejoice
ḫalābu, cover
ḫamat, aid
ḫamṭu, *ḫanṭu*, swift
ḫarādu, be victorious (?)
ḫarrānu, path, way (and *ḫarānu*)
ḫarū, to dig out
ḫaṭū, to sin
ḫiṭītu, sin
ḫubtu, plunder
ḫurāṣu, gold

Ṭ

ṭābtu, the good
ṭābu, to be pleasant, to be good
ṭābu, good
ṭaḫū, to approach
ṭeḫū, to draw near, to approach
ṭēmu, understanding, news
ṭiṭṭu, clay
ṭubbu, joy, health

K

kabattu, liver
kabittu, mind
kakku, weapon, arms
kalālu, to fulfil
kalbu, dog
kalmatu, insect
kam, after ordinal numbers
kamāsu, *kamāru*, to take one's stand
kamū, to conquer, to take
kanāšu, to prostrate, to submit
kānu, to stand
karābu, be propitious, bless, be gracious
kāru, wall
kašādu, capture, approach, conquer;
ik-šú-us-su-nu-ti for *ik-šú-ud-su-nu-ti*
katāmu, cover
kibratu, plu. *kibrāti*, region
kidinu, protection
kima, according to, like
kīpu, governor
kirbu, midst
kirū, park, plantation
kišādu, bank of a river
kiššatu, hosts
kištu, wood
kitru, assistance, aid
kurmatu, nourishment
kušer, becoming

L

labāru, to be old
labāšu, to clothe
lapan, before
libbu, heart
limnu, evil
limuttu, evil

lišānu, tongue, speech
lubultu, clothing

M

ma'adiš, *ana ma'adiš*, in great numbers
ma'adu, much
ma'ādu, to swarm, to be many
ma'diš, much
mada(t)tu, tribute
magāru, to be favourable, to favour, to obey
maḫāru, to receive
maḫāṣu, to smite, I_2 *imdaḫḫiṣ*, to fight
maḫazu, city, fortified-city
maḫḫūr, forward
maḫru, first, former
makātu, to fall, I_2 (*i-tu-kut* for *imtakut*) idem, III_1 to overthrow
mala, as many as
malāku, to counsel
malū, to fill
mama, any
mamītu, oath
mana, maneh
mandatu, gift
manma, any
manū, to number, to count
markasu, cord
marṣu, sick
mārtu, daughter
māru, II_1 to send
māru, son
maṣartu, a guard, watchman, observation
mašāru, II_1 to leave
maškanu, station, place
mašku, skin
maštītu, a drink
maṣū, to find
mašū, to forget
mātu, to die
mātu, land
me, enclitic particle
mētiku, course (comp. *etēku* and *mitiku*)
migru, darling
milammu, lustre
milku, counsel
mīni, how?
miṣru, territory
mitiku, progress (comp. *metiku*)
mītu, the dead
mū plu. *mē*, water
muḫḫu, top part
mušarkis, doer (from *rakāsu*)
mušpalu, depth
mūṣu, an exit
mušu, night
mūtu, death

N

nabalu, dry land, island
nabālu, to destroy
nabnītu, creation
nabū, to call, name
nadānu, to give
nadū, cast down
nakaru, foe, enemy
nakāru, destroy, lay waste
nakāsu, to cut down
nakiru, enemy
nalbašu, garment
namāru, to be bright
namriru, brilliance
napištu, life
narāmu, beloved
narāru, help
narkabtu, plu. chariot
nāru, river, canal
nasāḫu, drive away
našāku, to kiss
naṣāru, to keep, observe, keep watch, guard
našāšu, to move (?) p. 80, line 23
našū, to lift up
nazāzu, to stand (still), to station
nīḫu, peaceful, fem. *nihtu*
nindaggara, see *magāru*

nīru, yoke
nišu, people, men
nūru, light

S

saḫāpu, to cast down
saḫāru, III_2 to surround
sakāpu, to cast down
salū, to pray
sapānu, to overcome
sikkuru, bolt
sīmtu, insignia
sippu, threshold
sisū, horse
sittu, rest
sūḳu, street
surratu, sedition

P

padanu, way
pagru, corpse
paḳādu, to grant, to appoint
palāḫu, to fear
palū, year of reign
panū, face, former
parṣu, command
parū, mule
parzillu, iron
pašāḫu, be at rest
pašāru, to annul
paṭāru, to release
paṭru, dagger
pētū, porter
piḫātu, prefect
piḳittu, appointment
pitū, to open
pū, mouth
puluḫtu, fear
purussū, decision
pūtu, face, entrance

Ṣ

ṣabātu, to take, to grasp, to set forth
ṣābē kidinni, temple-servant
ṣābu, warrior, servant, soldier, man
ṣalmu, image
ṣalū, II_1 beseech
ṣamādu, to yoke
ṣānu, II_1 to adorn, to favour (or *za'ānu*)
ṣarāḫu, IV_1 was angry
ṣātu, *ūm ṣi'āte*, days of old
ṣeḫēru, to be young
ṣiḫru, small
ṣiru, a plain
ṣīru, noble
ṣīruššun, against them
ṣubātu, garment

Ḳ

ḳabal tāmtim, midst of the sea
ḳablu, fight
ḳabū, *ḳibū*, to speak, utter, say
ḳakḳadu, head
ḳakḳaru, place, ground
ḳapādu, to plan
ḳāpu, to entrust to
ḳarābu, to draw near; a battle
ḳāšu, to present
ḳātu, hand
ḳibītu, to command
ḳibū, to speak

R

rabū, great
rakābu, to ride
rakāsu, to bind (and comp. *mušarkis*)
rakbu, messenger
ramānišu, himself
ramū, to place
rāmu, to love, III/II_1 incline unto compassion
rapšu, broad
rašū, to grant, show
rašubtu, might

rēšu, head, summit
rīmu, grace
riksu, bond
rittu, hand
rubū, prince, fem. *rubātu*, princess
rūḳu, distant
rukūbu, carriage

Š

ša, as (it appeareth), who
šaʾālu, to ask
šabāru, to shatter
šadū, *satu*, mountain
šaḫāṭu, to strip
šakānu, to set, to place
šaknu, governor
šaḳū officer, see *šupāru*
šalālu, to carry off, to plunder
šalāmu, to be well, to prosper
šalāṭu, to pierce
šallatu, spoil, booty
šalmiš, peacefully
šalpūtu, misfortune
šamū, heaven
šanītu, time, repetition
šanū, another
šanū, declare, II$_1$ to inform
šapāḫu, to spread
šapāru, *sapāru*, to send
šaplū, lower
šarāḳu, to grant
šarāpu, to burn
šarratu, queen
šarru, constr. *šar*, king
šarrūtu, royalty
šašmu, battle
šaṭāru, to write
šatū, to drink
šēlibu, fox
šemū, to hear (and *šimū*)
šēpu, foot
šibbu, girdle
šimtu, fate
šimiru, a ring
šimū, to hear, see *šemū*
šipru, a dispatch
šiptu, incantation
šipu, foot (see *šēpu*)
šīru, flesh (heart), body
šubtu, constr. *šubat*, dwelling, seat
šuḳalulu, to swing
šulmu, peace, safety, well
šumma, if
šumu, name
šuparšaḳu (or better *šūt-šaḳē*), general
šupāru, ruler
šurbū, exalted
šūru, ox
šūtu, belonging to, see *šupāru*
šūturu, mighty (comp. *atāru*)

T

tabāku, to pour out
taḫazu, battle
taḫtū, overthrow
takālu, to trust
tamāḫu, to seize, to hold
tamartu, gift
tāmtu, *tāmdu*, sea
tāru, return, to turn, to fall; II$_1$ add
tenišētu, mankind
tēslītu, *tešlītu*, prayer
tibū, to rise, to come
tibūtu, the advance
tidūku, warrior
tillu, pit
tukultu, help

CORRIGENDA

Page 14, l. 11, for עֶרֶשׂ read עֶרֶשׂ.

„ 15, l. 9, for אַרְבַּץ read אַרְבַּע.

„ 16, § 16, l. 6, for contraction read harmony.

„ 19, § 19, l. 8, for [cuneiform] read [cuneiform]; l. 11, for [cuneiform] read [cuneiform]; and for [cuneiform] read [cuneiform]; l. 12, for transscription read transcription.

„ 23, l. 3, for [cuneiform] read [cuneiform]; also l. 4.

„ 24, 4, l. 1, for in read is.

„ 26, § 37, l. 12, for [cuneiform] read [cuneiform]; for [cuneiform] read [cuneiform].

„ 31, l. 2, for [cuneiform] read [cuneiform]; l. 4, for [cuneiform] read [cuneiform].

„ 33, l. 6, for [cuneiform] read [cuneiform].

„ 37, l. 9, for [cuneiform] read [cuneiform].

„ 39, § 55, l. 5, for [cuneiform] read [cuneiform].

„ 42, § 61, l. 9, for [cuneiform] read [cuneiform].

„ 43, l. 24, for *ibnikunā* read *ibnikunū*.

„ 44, l. 3, for [cuneiform] read [cuneiform].

„ 49, § 78, l. 11, for [cuneiform] read [cuneiform].

„ 53, l. 4, for [cuneiform] read [cuneiform].

„ 55, § 96, l. 5, before [cuneiform] insert [cuneiform].

„ 62, l. 4, for [cuneiform] read [cuneiform].

„ 64, l. 2, for [cuneiform] read [cuneiform].

„ 67, l. 29, for left read lift.